the fantastic salon

Alan Austin-Smith

TFH Publishing
London

This book is dedicated to Carolyn Field

Although it is my name on the front of this book and it is me that you see performing live at our seminars, the often-unseen hero of the Fantastic Hairdresser Company is my business partner Carolyn.

Her unfailing belief in my creativity gives me the strength to get out there and do what I do.

Thank you is not enough

The Fantastic Hairdresser Company Ltd
Barley Mow Centre, 10 Barley Mow Passage
Chiswick, London W4 4PH

First published in 2007

Editor: Carolyn Field

Design & creative: bluw creative

Printed by: Steffprint Ltd

A catalogue record of this book is available from the British Library
ISBN No.0-9546083-4-8
Printed in the UK

Welcome to The Fantastic Salon!

My first book 'The Fantastic Hairdresser', is aimed at the individual hairdresser and was based upon the common factors I discovered from observing and working with 'fantastic' hairdressers all around the world.

'The Fantastic Boss' - my second book, is ideal for anyone in a leadership or coaching position, dealing mainly with understanding the key leadership qualities such as communication, motivation and self-management.

And now - 'The Fantastic Salon' - written specifically for salon owners or people who have overall control of a salon.

This book is based upon a principle that I teach called 'the five pillars'.

Simply put, if your salon was being held up by 5 pillars, like a Greek temple, then all 5 pillars would have to be the same size - they would all have to be strong enough to support your business.

We often talk about this in terms of the business foundations – if your foundations are weak, then so will your business be. However, I prefer this mental image as it also suggests that if the pillars are both strong and tall then your business will rise above the rest – it will be the best!

The 5 pillars are:

Revolutionary strategies

This is where I will show you how to develop a strategy – a map of how to get to where you want to get to. Running a business is like going on a journey.

Firstly, you need to know where you are starting from and then where you are going.

Once you know both of these things, you can plan out how to get there.

A focus on profit

I often hear salon owners complaining that they have high sales but low profit.

This is where I will show you how to set targets for your business that focus on the profit you need and desire. From there, we'll look at how to break those targets down so that you can make good profitable business decisions on things like pricing, staffing levels, opening hours, etc.

A committed team

Of course to achieve your goals, you need to have a committed team of people working with you. However, the biggest problem is in motivating your team to be committed to what you want them to do, as of course people are only really committed to what they want to do.

In this part of the book I will show how to establish a common focus for the team, that they help create and so become committed to.

Delighted clients

Are you just giving the good service that frankly most clients would expect from you or are you WOW'ing people – delighting your clients rather than just serving them?

Here we will look at strategies and tools to keep your clients returning again and again, whilst spending more when they do but most important of all, because they want to - not because they have been sold to!

Unique marketing

Finally, we will look at the key principles of marketing your business successfully and cost-effectively, in order to achieve a business reputation that will give you the growth you desire.

Identifying your message, making sure that it is unique and then getting that message to the right people, will all be covered here - enabling you to create a unique marketing strategy for your business.

Ok, all you have to do now is get stuck in – enjoy!

Have fun,

Alan

ACKNOWLEDGEMENTS

Some big thank you's:

First of all to our 'fantastic' customers – some of you are new, however many of you have been with us for many, many years – thank you for your loyalty, your understanding, your unfailing support and trust in what we do and most of all for being such lovely people. On behalf of the whole team here at the Fantastic Hairdresser Company can I say a huge thanks for helping to make our job loads of fun.

To all the 'fantastic salons' that have helped contribute to this book – far too many to mention – I have learnt so much from you over the years and I can only hope that I do your brilliance credit, by communicating it in such a way that helps our industry grow and prosper.

My wonderful family, my Mum and my Dad, both teachers and obviously a great inspiration for me, instilling the belief that to teach is to give the most important gift of all – I wish you were here to see me carrying the torch on.

My beautiful children - my heroes, my inspiration and my passion – Craig, Sam and Nathan – the best advice I can give you is to simply enjoy life and keep having fun, and when sometimes it's not so much fun, keep looking ahead to when it will be again – because it will!

Christine, it means so much to see you so happy now and Shelly, I am really proud of you and what you are achieving in your life.

Sometimes in your life, you meet special people – those people inspire you, excite you and give you the energy to live your life to its fullest. I am lucky enough to be surrounded by many such people in my circle of family and friends, but on the 14th of July 2007, I will marry the one person who constantly amazes and inspires me with her wonderful outlook on life and the way it should be lived.

I love you Anny and always will x

Ricky – you are amazing, you have bought my book to life with your brilliant graphics. Thank you and thanks also to all the rest of the team at Bluw Creative - once again you have helped to create a 'fantastic' product.

Nique and Sam – thanks for all the work you both do to make my life easier – I really appreciate it and so do all our customers

Finally, Carolyn – a wonderful friend, a 'fantastic mum', my business partner and the person who keeps it all together here at the fantastic hairdresser company.

Thank you so much for making sure that this book reads the way it does – the tireless and thankless job of editing and proofing a book like this is actually the key to making it great – and it is great – so thank you!

HOW TO USE THIS BOOK

As with all my books, they are designed to be used in many ways.

If you are a reader, then go ahead and enjoy reading it for the first time from beginning to end.

However, I would strongly recommend that you still take it in small chunks – maybe one chapter at a time, which then gives you time to stop, put the book down for a few moments, make some notes about what you have got from that chapter and then most importantly of all, what action you are going to take.

If you are not much of a reader, then just dip in and out of the book.

Flip through and find something that appeals or that you think is important for you. Just open it there and read – you will soon know if you need to go back a few pages to understand more about what you just read, or whether you just want to read on.

You will end up reading the whole book one way or another but not necessarily from the beginning to the end.

As you will find with all of my books,

this is a valuable teaching tool.

If you are using it to help someone else learn, I suggest that you ask them to read one chapter and then sit down with you to discuss what they learnt from that chapter. This will automatically start up a discussion between you which will be an invaluable learning for both of you.

Then do the same again for the next chapter and so on. It goes without saying that you would have to have read the same chapter as them in order for this to work properly.

You will find action pages at the end of each chapter. Of course, it's up to you – I know it doesn't appeal to everybody but I really would suggest that you use these pages to reflect on what you have learnt and identify areas that you want to take action on. It will increase the effectiveness of the book dramatically.

Be confident to write in this book - make it yours. Jot your thoughts and comments at the side of the pages.

I love it when I see my book stuffed in someone's bag - all beaten up, written in and well used. None of my books are the sort of books you read and then put back on the shelf forever. By the way, don't lend your book - not only might you not see it again but as I have already said, you will need it again and again - either for reference, motivation or re-direction. So make sure you keep your hands on it!

Finally the most important part - which I will talk more about later but,

it is no good reading this book or any book, without taking action.

Be confident in that what you find in the following pages will work – if you know anything about me, then you may also know that I have been a part of this wonderful industry since the age of sixteen - kicking off my career at Vidal Sassoon in London. I have been a trainee, a stylist, creative director, manager, educator and salon owner. I worked with L'Oreal for 6 years, firstly as a technician and then in management. And for the last 18 years, I have been running a consultancy and training company with my business partner Carolyn Field, specialising in the salon industry.

When I work with a salon business - as a business consultant, everything is confidential – of course it is. However, that does not stop me from telling you that there are common characteristics within both the successful salons and the ones that are struggling.

In fact, after having gone through our records and realising that I have sat down with more than 1,500 salon owners over the last 20 years, looking at their business intimately, seeing everything there is to see - the truth - not bar bullshit - those common characteristics start to shine out like a beacon.

However you come into contact with the Fantastic Hairdresser Company be it through our books, live seminars, our ground breaking 'Ambassador Programme' or from using our website – www.fantastichairdresser.com,

you can be confident that everything we discuss or teach is based upon real proven success.

Everything we say is based upon real people - just like you - the salon owners, hairdressers, beauty therapists etc., – the fantastic performers working in fantastic salons that hold the secrets to success.

I have always worked on a simple principle: Find people who are successful at what you want to do and then find out what they are doing! That's what I have been doing for the last 30 years or so and all I do now is tell everybody what I have learnt - through our books, our training and with our on-line Academy.

Everything works! It has been proven. However, sometimes it doesn't – it doesn't work if you don't take action! Learning without action is pointless - nothing will change.

If you want change – change something!

1

WHAT MAKES A FANTASTIC SALON?

BALANCE

PASSION

CONSISTENCY

Ok then, here we go – So what is that makes a 'fantastic' salon?

You know when you walk down a busy street looking for a restaurant – it doesn't matter where you are in the world, we have all had the same experience – some restaurants will be busy, some will be empty and one or two will be heaving.

Why does this happen – it can't just be about the food – if that were the case how on earth did some of the well known fast food chains become so successful?

The 'X' factor

It's those magic ingredients, the 'X' factors and all those other intangible things that make such a huge difference.

Of course it is no different in the salon industry – how can one salon be empty with just a few team members sitting around doing nothing, whilst another salon maybe just a few doors down the road is full to capacity with people spending plenty of money?

Well, as I have already mentioned, I have sat down with over 1500 salon owners over the last 20 years and seen what they are doing in detail, intimately - remember I see everything - and I see the truth. No bar bullshit here, people are paying a lot of money to bring me into their business, telling me lies would be a bit daft!

Common characteristics

What starts to happen is that you begin to notice common characteristics. All the successful salons – the fantastic ones – are doing similar things and of course, I see the not so fantastic salons doing all the same things wrong as well. Put these together and a 'fantastic' pattern starts to emerge.

Modelling

I have always believed in something called 'modelling' - a technique used by many top sports and business people. It is very simple and makes so much sense – watch individuals or companies that are performing at the highest level find out what they are doing differently to everyone else and then model it (yes that does mean copy!)

Add your own creativity and personality to what you learn, however you must understand that these people are not successful through luck alone and however insignificant the differences sometimes seem, they are making a difference – so give it a go.

There are many things that 'fantastic salons' are doing that is different to the normal salon out there. In this book we will look at the things that I believe will have the greatest impact on your business, however I really want to focus firstly on three areas that I believe are at the heart of a fantastic salon – you could call them the foundations if you like.

Passion

The first is very important to me – I fell in love with this wonderful business when I was 16 years old, and although I am no longer a hairdresser, I still can't get away from it. Passion drives the salon industry – it is the passion, which keeps people working in this business and it is certainly the passion, which helps some people stand out from the crowd.

Balance

This is an interesting one – a successful business is a balanced one. For example, it will be team orientated but not a push over, it will train, motivate and support people in their development, but will not keep hold of a disruptive team member for too long. It will understand that it needs to make a profit, but will not sacrifice service standards in the pursuit of that goal.

Think about it, do you keep people in your salon that you should've let go of a long time ago? Do you give great service but not make enough profit? Then you have an imbalance.

Consistency

I often liken the salon industry to San Francisco – an exciting, vibrant, passionate city that is full of creative energy, but that also has the San Andreas Fault running through it.

Our exciting, vibrant and passionate business has it's own fault line running through and it can be just as disastrous as an earthquake might be to San Francisco – it is called 'inconsistency' and if it is running through your business like the San Andreas Fault then I guarantee you will never achieve the success you desire.

So let's start here then – A Fantastic Salon...

Keeps the passion
Balances the business
Does it right – consistently!

Passionate systems

A long time ago, I remember learning something that had a dramatic impact on how I saw our business. Interestingly it is having just as big an impact on me today but in a completely different way.

I was attending a Tom Peters seminar and he talked about something called 'passionate systems'.

"You can't have passion without systems or systems without passion" he said. "You must have both!"

You can have all the passion in the world but if you do not have the systems, standards and procedures in place, your flame of passion will be blown out. Equally, he argued that there are many companies with all the systems in place – but no passion. That isn't going to work either.

You need both

As I listened to this, it was immediately clear where we generally go wrong in the salon industry – bucket loads of passion with no systems!!

Now of course I wasn't the only one to realise this – manufacturers, distributors, educational companies, industry business gurus and other salon owners were all trying to get the salon industry to be more organised and efficient, with the right procedures and benchmarks in place to ensure success.

This has been happening over the last 20 years and although there is still plenty yet to be done here, in general we have done a great a job over that period.

In fact, when I think back to what Tom Peters told me all those years ago I now realise that there is still something critical to be taken out of that principle – you can't have passion without systems or systems without passion.

Sometimes I feel that in our pursuit of becoming an efficient business we are forgetting what that business is – hairdressing – a creative, fun, exciting and passionate business.

A fantastic salon
KEEPS THE PASSION

Are we in danger of ending up with great systems but losing the passion?

Well I think we are! This is only my personal opinion, however I would remind you of what I base all my views on – thousands of other hairdresser's views. Hairdressers – not manufacturers, distributors, educators etc., (who will all tell you what is 'wrong' with 'hairdressers' if you are prepared to listen to them) no, I listen to the people who we need to operate at the highest level, in order to get the results we want from our business.

This is the sort of stuff I hear:

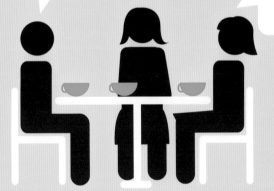

"Why can't I just do great hair?"

"It's all about money these days"

"All my boss ever tells me is what I'm 'not' doing"

"More retail, sell more colour, do more clients, increase your average client spend. What happened to being a fantastic hairdresser and making people look and feel great?"

"We have so many systems here I think they will start measuring how long we spend going to the toilet next!"

"I never understand what they are going on about – percentages, average docket and stuff – and as for all those computer print out sheets – what is that all about?"

"I just agree with them and nod my head until the next time – it's what they want – then I can get on with doing the job that I love!"

STOP!!

If you are listening to those comments and thinking to yourself, yep, that's right, that's all I ever hear from my lot – bloody hairdressers!! - Then you are missing the point.

Is it about money? **YES!**

Do we need more than just great hair? **YES!**

Do we need more product/colour/treatment sales etc,
to increase the average client spend? **YES!**

Do we need to measure performance and give feedback? **YES!**

Should we share business information? **YES!**

Of course we need to do all those things and more but what we need more than anything is a motivated team of people who love what they are doing with a passion, because that is where the results we need will come from. The best-laid battle plan won't work if the troops that have to carry it out are de-motivated.

We need to continue to improve our business skills and knowledge, continue to implement the systems and standards needed for success – but not at the expense of the passion – that special energy that lies at the heart of any successful salon or hairdresser.

We must keep the passion!

Balance is the key to nature – it is critical for survival – male/female, yin/yang, work/life etc. Well I feel that it is just as critical in business. I watch many businesses swinging from one extreme to another constantly – if they would just find the middle ground then they would find life so much easier.

Let me give you some examples:

Sometimes customers of ours explain that they are not going to do any business training currently as they feel that they have lost focus on the hairdressing. Wait a minute, isn't this just what I've been talking about in the previous pages? NO – what I was talking about was keeping the focus on hairdressing whilst developing the business – not instead of. I guarantee that within a couple of years that same customer is calling us back because they have lost direction and the business is suffering.

Here is another common one – we have learnt the importance of teamwork over the last few years – the importance of nurturing and supporting the team. We praise, encourage, say thank you, give gifts, are understanding over personal issues, flexible with time when needed etc. However do you sometimes feel like your team are taking advantage of this?

You know what I mean, it's when someone begs you for a Saturday off to go to a friend's wedding and you decide to let them go, only to have them make some excuse for not staying late one night at the salon when you've asked them to help you out.

How about the balance between sales and profit? Are you profitable with low sales? Or more commonly today, do you have high sales with low profit, stuffing money into the till but having nothing left at the end?

What follows are the key areas where I believe that you must have balance in the business for you to have a Fantastic Salon – there are obviously lots of other areas that need to be balanced, however these are the ones that I see causing the most problems. Throughout the book we will discuss all of these in more detail, but I want you to start thinking about how these relate to you now.

A fantastic salon
HAS A BALANCED BUSINESS

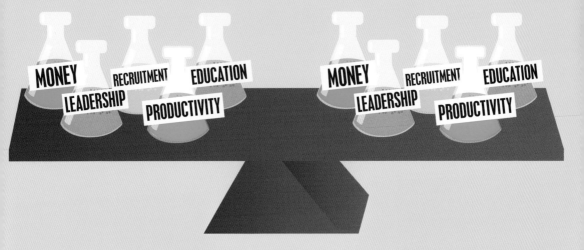

Recruitment

There are two types of balance to look at here. The first is between nice people and talented people. We all know that there are many talented people in this industry who are not team players, cause problems with colleagues, can be moody, upset clients etc – but they are talented with hair. Equally, there are some lovely people who do not have what it takes to do great hair.

When you are recruiting, make sure you don't sacrifice one or the other - you need both lovely people who do great hair. However the one thing I would say, is that it is generally easier to train someone to do better hair work than it is to make them nicer people!

The other balance you need to look for is a balance of roles within the team – we will look at this more later.

Education

Business development and client care or hairdressing ability – BOTH!

Leadership

In the old days, leadership was so simple – 'do as I say or there's the door'. Of course it doesn't work like that anymore for many reasons, apart from the moral and ethical issues, it just wouldn't work – in this industry people no longer fear losing their jobs as they used to, they know they can just go and get another one. In most countries, unemployment in the salon business is almost zero. Therefore, we discovered teamwork and all the good stuff that goes along with it.

Well if an autocratic leadership style is at one end of the see-saw then I find that many salon owners have gone right over to the opposite end with their teamwork principles. Many owners have become too soft, too afraid of upsetting people in case they left and ended up being taken for granted by people who might love working for them – but aren't getting results!

We need to be somewhere in the middle with teamwork, support, empowerment etc., - all within easy reach, whilst also being close enough to the other end of the see-saw - taking a tough stand when needed.

Productivity

Of course we need to be busy, of course we need to fit in as many clients as we can, but unless you are at the cheap and cheerful end of the market, we also have to provide a fantastic experience. Don't sacrifice the experience by packing clients in, but equally it is no good giving an amazing experience if there are not enough clients to pay the bills – BALANCE!

Money

As I have already suggested and will look at in much more detail in chapter six, the balance here must be between sales and profit. It is no good boasting about how much money you take if there is little or no profit left at the end – by the way – when I talk about profit I come from a business point of view not just an accountant's point of view.

Most accountants view profit as what it shows on the P&L statement. However unless you are a limited company this will not take into account the salon owners' salary/drawings. By the way, even if you are a limited company a good accountant will probably show a minimum salary in the P&L whilst listing the rest as dividend, which is actually much the same as a sole trader/partnership.

Now, if your salary has just allowed you to buy your third home and pay for your Aston Martin DB9, then I guess we can safely assume that you are very profitable. However, you are choosing to take that profit as salary. I think we all know that this would be the exception to the rule though – most salon owners are taking a fair salary out of the business that is in line with the job they are doing. What this means though is that you must add this into the P&L to make any sense of what the business is actually achieving.

I hear this comment all the time – "my accountant says I made X profit – but I don't know where it is!" Quite often the amount shown under drawings/dividend is remarkably similar to the profit shown in the P&L statement – you did make X profit, but you took it as salary.

So when you ask yourself if you have a good sales/profit balance, remember that your salary is an expense and must be offset against the profit.

I often ask this question of my audiences;

"I am not asking you whether you do it right in your salon – of course you do – what I am asking you is, are you doing it right – consistently?"

That's the big question that we have to address.

Consistency is an issue in any business, but when we are talking about creative people offering a service, it becomes a major issue. Think about it – our business is one of very few where creative people come face to face with the customer, actually providing the service. The chef is in the kitchen, the designer is not selling clothes in the shop, the artist does not own the gallery, the performer has a recording company to sell the CD and the author is not serving behind the desk in the bookshop.

The 'just a hairdresser' syndrome

I often wonder if that is why we get such bad press – it is not just hairdressers who can be ego led; not always interested in academic subjects or current events and politics, have 'party' high on their list of priorities, as well as not always being the most organised people. In fact, I find many creative people I meet are equally as good as all the hairdressers I have met, at showing some of the worst tendencies of creative people.

By the way, I am not excusing some of these things, just simply pointing out that it is not just hairdressers who can be like this – however most members of the public do not come into contact with a creative person every 6 weeks so they attribute it all to 'hairdressers' – specifically with that 'roll of the eyes' we have all seen.

I think we all want to get rid of that 'just a hairdresser' syndrome as I call it. I have certainly fought against it throughout my career. We need to have pride in ourselves and what we do, to understand that what we do every day, believe it or not has social worth - particularly in these days of increased stress.

I hear so many stories that prove this – this one is recent: A woman who had just come out of an abusive relationship with extremely low self esteem.

She visited a new hairdresser who during the consultation remarked on what a lovely face she had.

The client started to cry. She realised that nobody had said anything like that to her in years – she now says that it was a turning point for her. Something as simple as that helped her to begin her recovery.

'JUST A HAIRDRESSER SYNDROME' CURE

Have you ever thought about how many great relationships we are responsible for, simply because someone felt more confident about themselves after a visit to your salon? How many people are in their dream job because they visited you before the interview?

We are not 'just a hairdresser'. I am in no doubt about that – that is why I love Vivienne Mackinder's films – the 'not just a hairdresser' series. They are so inspiring and get a fantastic message across about what we can achieve in this wonderful business of ours. Meanwhile, here is the point to all of this;

The only people who can change other people's perceptions of the hairdressing industry are: Ourselves!

Inconsistency

I believe that the single biggest problem we face in this business is inconsistency. Inconsistency in the experience we provide from day to day, inconsistency in leadership, inconsistency in marketing, in education, in business management, in attitude and motivation and most of all inconsistency in following through and taking action on the things we need to.

We talk a great fight in this business, but we are not always as great at putting all that talk into action.

We have all started things – and the crazy thing is, we have started things that actually work, that are making a difference – and then somehow those actions get lost along the way. You start having regular meetings held in a fun and enjoyable way that motivates the team and then somewhere along the line – it is difficult to pinpoint exactly where or when - you slip back into the same old mundane meetings where you just read things from a list of items and bore the pants off the team.

I hear this all the time – salon owners telling me, "we always used to"... Or, "we did that once – it was really good". Once? If it was really good, why only ONCE?

Do it right - consistently

I judged the Global Salon Business Awards in 2006 and vividly remember one particular entry. This salon was clearly a good business with high turnover and good profit. It was doing all the right stuff both with the team and in terms of the service the client was getting. They did loads of good marketing as well, however we were having a problem with judging it. You see the brief we had been given was to be looking for something innovative, something different – all the entrants were great salons, they were all doing amazing things, so the winners had to be doing that extra something.

Our problem was that although this salon was doing lots of good stuff, there was nothing innovative or different about what they were doing. If I listed for you some of the marketing they were doing, you wouldn't particularly say "wow - that's a good idea". For example; giving out balloons to the kids outside the salon on a Saturday morning, hair party evenings, client research, PR in the local press etc – normal stuff.

Then all of a sudden I got it – this salon **was unique,** it was doing something different, even though what it was doing was fairly basic - tried and tested methods of marketing the business, keeping clients happy and motivating the team etc., but they were doing that 'normal stuff' consistently: Hair parties **every week,** giving things out to the kids outside the salon – **every Saturday morning,** featured in the local press **weekly,** etc.

I realised this salon was still operating as if it were a new salon - doing all the stuff that everyone does to get clients through the door when they first open, even though this salon had been open for 7 years!

It was their consistency that made them unique!

Model Success

Learn from individuals or companies that are performing at the highest level to find out what they are doing differently to everyone else and then try it yourself.

Keep the Passion

In your pursuit of becoming an efficient business make sure you remember what that business is – hairdressing – a creative, fun, exciting and passionate business.

Be careful you do not end up with great systems in your business, but no passion!

A Balanced Business

You can put all the correct ingredients in a bowl to make a cake, but if you have the wrong measurements, it won't be a good cake!

It's the same with your business – it must have a balance.

Do it right consistently

The question isn't whether you are doing it right – the question is whether you are doing it right consistently, day after day – time after time?

Choose 3 goals from this chapter that you can take immediate action on:

2

THE 'FANTASTIC' PRINCIPLES

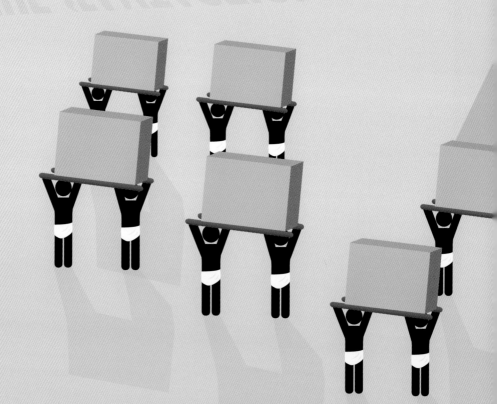

If this is the first time you have had anything to do with the Fantastic Hairdresser Company then you need to understand some of our core principles – they are the foundations our company is built upon and underpin everything we do. All our books, live seminars and training systems are based upon these principles.

If you are a customer of ours already or have read some of my other books, you could skip this chapter, although I wouldn't if I were you as I have added stuff that is relevant to this particular book - especially here and also in 'fly test' pages.

However, it is also because I believe that you will still learn something from it, even if you have been through this type of content before. People often ask me how I keep myself motivated. Well the answer is - the same as anyone else does. I read, I learn and I attend many live events, but I am slightly embarrassed to admit that probably the biggest motivation is constantly listening to myself go through these principles as I speak to an audience. I will even admit that sometimes I think to myself; personally I'm not doing what I tell you to do – now that is a great kick up the backside for me, let me assure you!

I think what I am trying to say here, is that even if you have heard me talk about these principles before, I still think that you can learn something by reading through them again – even if you only pick up one thing, that's got to be worth it hasn't it?

The 50% rule

This one really is the basis of everything we do. It's very simple, I believe that 50% of what makes someone fantastic at their job, has nothing to do with their job!

Would you agree that 50% of what makes a fantastic hairdresser has nothing to do with a pair of scissors?

50% is to do with a pair of scissors of course, but most hairdressers have that 50% - It is the other stuff that makes the difference; communication skills, confidence, attitude, motivation, customer delight, etc.

Fantastic bin men

I was having one of those strange conversations at a barbeque last year along the lines of; 'bin men ain't what they used to be!' One woman interrupted though, saying that her bin men were fantastic (yes she even used that word). What did she mean – was she marvelling at the way they picked up her bags of rubbish and threw them in the back of the truck? I don't think so. I think she was talking about them being happy, that they said good morning, closed the gate etc.

On another occasion, I was about to do a coaching session with three surgeons. I must admit I did have some fears about what on earth I was going to do with them but a visit I made to an elderly relative in hospital a few weeks before I was due to do the session, gave me confidence. When I asked her how she was doing and if she was being looked after ok, she said "Oh yes. Everybody's lovely and my surgeon is fantastic." (that word again).

Again – what was she talking about? Had they let her sit up and watch? Was it the skill and dexterity of the surgeon she was commenting on, how efficient he was? – Of course not – that, we would expect. No, she was telling me about how friendly he was, how caring and understanding he had been.

She was having a routine operation but as a 78 year old who had never had an operation before, she was understandably very apprehensive. You can imagine can't you, that some surgeons would be very dismissive of her fears - just telling her not to worry - that it was just routine. Not this surgeon. She understood my relative's fears and spent time reassuring her, caring about her as a human being, chatting about her family etc., – she didn't just see her as her 'next patient!'

Now that's a fantastic surgeon – my fears had gone too, I realised that even surgeons work to the same rule.

50% of what makes you fantastic at your job has nothing to do with your job!

It doesn't matter what job you do, from bin men to surgeons, this rule applies.

What makes a great cab driver, waitress, foreman, etc?

Just one small point here, but it is important to me - as you know from earlier comments about passion. Sometimes people in their enthusiasm to agree with me on this, point out that they think it is more than 50%, saying that it is nearer 70 or 80%.

I do understand what they are trying to say but I never let that pass – "No" I say, "it's 50%, otherwise we start to diminish the 'hair' 50% and we must never do that – we mustn't forget who we are and what we do, otherwise we lose the passion"

The fantastic boss

To finish on this principle then, let me also point out that 50% of what makes a fantastic boss has got nothing to do with admin, stock control, lunch rotas, the till, etc.

The fantastic salon

In addition, 50% of what makes a fantastic salon has nothing to do with just doing great hair – it's exactly the same – that's what this book is all about – the other stuff that you need to do as well as great hair, to have a truly fantastic salon.

FANTASTIC AT YOUR JOB
AWARDS

I've always believed that you must have some idea of the direction you are heading in life, but even more importantly, and something that is often missed is that you have to know where you are starting from.

The Total Life Concept helps you identify where you are at the moment, and more importantly, where you should be.

This wonderful tool started life as the Total Product Concept, a marketing tool that I learnt from Tom Peters. However, the more I used it, the more I realised that it wasn't just about marketing, or even business. It was about everything. That's when I named it TLC - the Total Life Concept.

It starts at the centre with the 'core' of what you do. For example the 'core' reason a hairdressing salon exists is to cut peoples' hair. A hotel is there because people need a bed and restaurants are for eating in.

EXPECTED

Then it moves out to the next ring, with 'expected'.

I go to your salon for a haircut, but I expect a certain level of service. I expect to be able to have colour on my hair if I want, to have a coffee, to be offered a magazine etc.

How many people do you know that stop here in their life. They do what is expected - but no more. The person who finishes work on the dot, regardless of what needs to be done. The stylist who doesn't think they need to learn anymore, or who doesn't think it's their job to help keep the salon clean, has stopped in 'expected'.

I was discussing business training with a salon owner who came out with a line I will always remember. He didn't see that he needed any training, as in his own words:

"We are no worse than anyone else in this town!"

Isn't that amazing? I am a very visual person and I already had a whole marketing campaign going on in my mind - posters at key sites, banners in the window, newspaper adverts all carrying the line "Come to us, we are no worse than anyone else!"

If anything sums up people stopping at "expected" then that line is it.

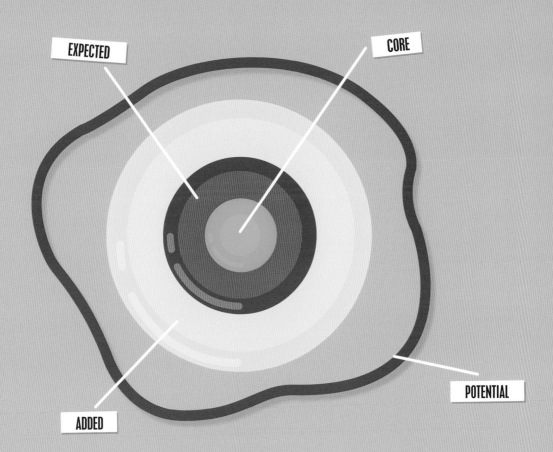

EXPECTED

CORE

ADDED

POTENTIAL

ADDED

The next ring is the 'added' part of the model. Going further than expected, taking that extra step, exceeding the expectations. We all know what this feels like when it happens to us. It's great.

"I expected a certain level of service - but wow, I didn't expect this!"

When any individual or company goes beyond expectations, they create a fantastic response.

I know a beauty therapist who sends thank you cards to all her new clients - It is not the company policy, she does it off her own back!

Interestingly when I discovered this person, she was working in a new salon, having started 6 months earlier with three other therapists. After 6 months, one of the four is consistently fully booked, whilst the other three sit around moaning that there are not enough clients. No prizes for guessing which one is fully booked!

Is this where the winners are? Well it certainly looks like it. But actually it's not. In fact if you are sitting in 'added', patting yourself on the back for all the great things that you do - you are actually in 'expected', and you probably don't even realise it.

POTENTIAL

It is this final part of the Total Life Concept where you find the winners 'Potential'. It's here where you ask: "What's next? Now what do I do?"

It's here where the key to survival is, in this ever changing world - Creativity.

As I have just said, many people are sitting around in 'added' feeling good about themselves because of what they do and how they do it. Not realising that what was once special - the service you provide, the way you deal with your clients, the hair work that you do, has now become the norm - expected.

The only way to stay ahead is to be constantly in 'potential'. Always moving, growing and learning - creatively looking for what's next.

THE STORY OF A KETTLE

You see, the model works from the outside in - A hotel somewhere, whilst in 'potential' (the outside) - decided to put kettles in all their rooms. The moment they did this, the kettle moved into the 'added' part of the model, with you the guest pleasantly surprised to find a kettle in your room.

But now, if you checked into a hotel tonight - you would 'expect' a kettle in your room.

So the kettle in a hotel room started it's life in 'potential', moved into 'added' and finished up in 'expected'.

THIS HAPPENS TO EVERYTHING!

Think about it and you will see I'm right. Everything starts with a creative idea, spends a period of time being unique, different, special, before eventually becoming the norm and ending up as expected. If you are not in 'potential', you are in 'expected' - standing still, in the one place you can't afford to be if you want to be successful today.

Finally think about why I changed the name to total LIFE concept. Look at relationships and see how that early excitement of 'potential' turns into a wonderful time of your life in 'added' but can become so boring and flat in 'expected'.

This model applies to all areas of your life - you have to spend as much time as you can in the outer circle to stay ahead of the game, to achieve the success that you want in each moment.

If you want change – change something

Responsibility – if it's to be, it's up to me:

Firstly it is important that you understand the difference between responsibility and blame or fault. Of course sometimes you are taking responsibility for the blame - "it was my fault". But there is a difference between the two.

Many people say to me that their boss doesn't respect them, doesn't communicate well, or doesn't have any time for them. Or I hear that their partner in life doesn't give them the love and affection that they would like.

Often these people are saying "it's not my fault." And maybe it isn't, but my question is always the same – do you want it to change? And if the answer is yes, then it is your responsibility to do something about it, even if it's not your fault.

"If you want change, change something"

The fly test:

We all need to do the fly test in certain areas of our life. So what is a fly test?

Picture a sunny day, you're in the kitchen and the back door is open. A fly flies through the door and into your kitchen. The window doesn't open and as the fly buzzes around your kitchen it sees through the window – blue sky, trees and grass. That's what I'm looking for it thinks, and heads straight for it.

Now you may be surprised to know that flies have no perception of glass! They don't cover it at fly school!! Smack......... it must be quite a shock; however the fly seems to recover quite well and continues buzzing around until it sees through the window - blue sky, trees and grass. Smack........ They don't learn too well these flies. In fact it will carry on doing this for hours if you let it. During this time if you don't want to swat it you will try to wave it towards the open door, but each time you get it close, it will turn and head straight back towards the window.

THE FLY TEST

The fly keeps repeating the behaviour that is getting it nowhere, whilst if it would just go in a different direction, the result it needs is just behind it.

So that's the fly test - repeating a behaviour that is getting us nowhere - over and over again.

We all need to take a fly test at certain times in our life; 'If you want change, change something'

How many people do you know that want changes in their life but are not prepared to change anything?

- People who want to stop smoking, but continue to put cigarettes in their mouth.

- People who want to lose weight, but continue to eat too much.

- People who want to get fit, but don't go to the gym.

- People who want to save money, but continue to spend more than they earn.

If you want change, change something.

People achieving success understand that they have to take responsibility. There are people standing beside the road of life with their thumbs out, waiting to be taken to where they want to go, whilst others are already driving there.

I feel as though our industry has to do a fly test

There are many things that we have learnt over the years that have improved the salon business dramatically, however there are also many things we have learnt that aren't working – that is understandable – part of the whole process of success is called failure.

Soichira Honda once said:

The 1% that we call success comes from the 99% that we call failure

However, this only works if you learn from the failure. Constantly repeating the things that don't work means it's time for the fly test!

A great example of this is the language we use sometimes in the salon.

Much of our business learning has come from the manufacturers and distributors over the last 20 years. This has been great as it has allowed us to develop our knowledge dramatically, at a reasonable cost, which in turn has helped us move the salon industry to where it is today.

However, much of the information was sourced from large company's Human Resource Departments (Don't you just hate that title - why can't we just be called people?)

That is why we have tools such as performance appraisals, retailing and why we talk to our people in percentages etc.

Language is a very powerful thing. It is one of the key ways we communicate to peoples' minds and if that language is not motivating – guess what – people won't be motivated.

Do a fly test – think about the types of things you say within your company when communicating with your team – ask yourself whether it is motivating for people in this industry and if not find an alternative way to say it. Here are some examples of what I mean;

- Performance reviews might become one to one's

- Staff meetings become team meetings

- Working for becomes working with

- Instead of using percentages – make it real – turn those figures into client count – only 2 out of ten clients having colour makes much more sense than a percentage figure.

- Scare sheets ?? – need I say more – if any of you are still using this description of a very useful and positive breakdown of someone's performance, please ask yourself what the title says about it.

Retailing

We have a great fly test to do here – we have put so much work and effort into developing this part of the business over the last 20 years or so, but in many cases we are still not getting results.

Why is this? I believe it is the whole concept of retail that we have introduced into the industry. Take my advice and stop retailing!

Let me give you some history. About 25 years ago, manufacturers and distributors started teaching hairdressers how to sell. However, the training was put together by the sales training department in those companies – sounds sensible enough and as always, hindsight is a wonderful thing – but it meant that we were being taught 'sales' techniques. I remember teaching people how to 'close the sale', 'overcome objections' and use 'alternative closes' etc. For many people the immediate reaction to much of this was

'I am not a sales person – I am a hairdresser'

Although much of this training has now changed, I think that the belief - 'all you want me to do is sell more' - still exists.

We stopped using the word 'sell'. We were told to use words like 'advise' and 'recommend'. Well as I used to say "Us hairdressers are not as stupid as you think, we know what you want, however you phrase it."

It is not just changing words that makes the difference and that is the same for all the examples earlier – it is no good changing the name of a scare sheet and still using it to scare people!

We have to change the whole attitude of what we are doing – retailers make money out of selling products – service providers make money out providing fantastic service.

Stop retailing and start being fantastic hairdressers

A great hairdresser sends people out of the door looking and feeling fantastic. We will discuss this in more detail later, however it is quite simple – the more people who leave your salon with colour in their hair and the right products in their bathroom - the more people there are out there looking and feeling fantastic.

One of the results of you doing your job really well is that you make more money.

Making money from selling products etc., is a result of doing your job well - not just doing your 'job'.

The next chapter goes into this whole 'fly test' issue in more depth by explaining a principle I use called the 'boardroom to the changing room'. It shows how we have to change the way we communicate with people in order to motivate them to get the results we all want.

Success pyramid

This is a model that I created after spending many years 'modelling' - studying successful people in all walks of life. Identifying with the people that I consider successful, looking at what it was they were doing and then pulling together the common characteristics that they all shared.

Success is at the peak of the pyramid which is obviously where we are going, but I want to start in the centre with 'learn'.

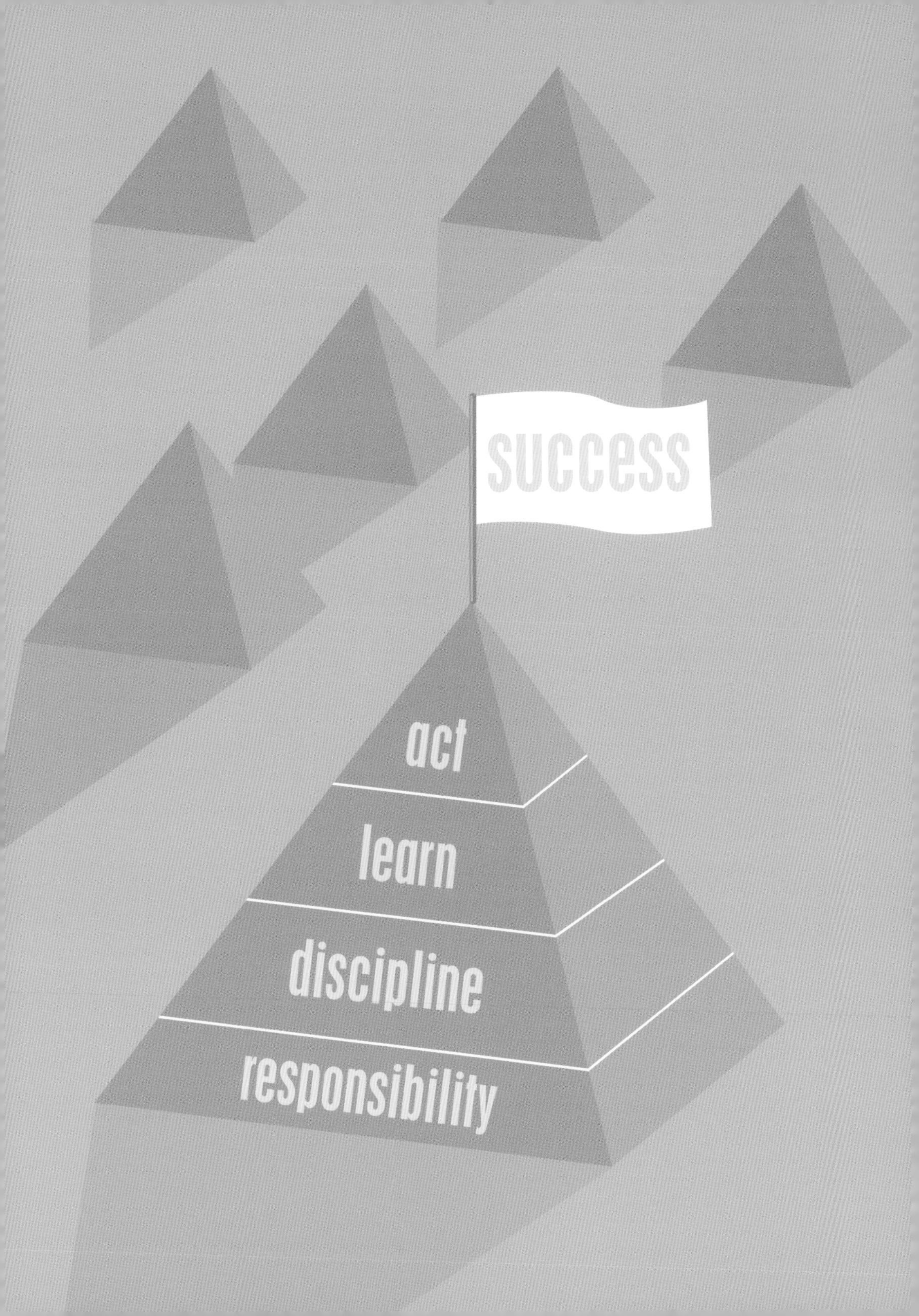
success
act
learn
discipline
responsibility

The first lesson I discovered is simply that you cannot just <u>learn</u> to be successful.

Everybody is doing it - reading books, magazines, going on courses, surfing the internet. So many people are committed to learning today but I fear that many people in their last moments of this life will be saying, "I did all that learning but nothing ever happened for me. Nothing changed."

"You cannot learn to be successful." What am I doing, talking myself out of business here?

Am I saying you should shut this book now and forget about it? Of course not. All I am saying is that learning on its own will not take you to success. You need to fill in the box above it with - action.

The population can quite easily be split into those who are taking the action they need to and those who are waiting for it to happen to them.

Have you ever read a book, or attended a course and learnt something that you knew was critical to you - that made you think – "That's me! I must do something about that" and then… taken no action? Well I've got my hand up here, have you?

It is the action that you take with what you learn that will get you to success, not just learning on its own. Sometimes when I am running a course, people ask me what time will we be finishing. I always say "around 5 o'clock" but what I should really say is, "Well I am finishing at about five but you're just starting!"

Learning isn't the last step, it's the first step.

So what about the other two slices of the pyramid? At the bottom is responsibility and then above it, discipline.

It all starts with responsibility - everything does

As we have already discussed, anything that anybody has ever achieved has only happened after they have taken responsibility first. However, having taken responsibility to make a change, you now need the discipline to keep it going.

Have you ever taken responsibility for your health or wealth? You know - it's when you decide to smoke less, drink less, exercise more, save more money etc. I'm sure you are already ahead of me here – It's one thing to take responsibility - to start those things, it's another to have the discipline to keep it going.

This is how the pyramid works: First you take responsibility for the action you need to take, then you have to have the discipline to keep taking that action. Learn more about the action and then you will take that action - in order to reach the peak of the pyramid.

The 50% rule

50% of what makes a fantastic salon, a fantastic hairdresser – in fact a fantastic anything – is all to do with the other stuff – communication, attitude, consistency, confidence, motivation, etc.

The Total Life Concept

Has your salon slipped into the 'expected' part of the model? All that great stuff you are doing has just become the norm – get out onto the edge and start learning, changing, innovating etc. to bring the WOW back.

The Fly Test

Do you need to take the fly test? Are there behaviours that you are repeating over and over again that are getting you nowhere?

The Success Pyramid

Do you need to take responsibility, or is it more discipline? Maybe you need more knowledge or need to just start taking action on the learning that you do – where are you on the success pyramid?

Choose 3 goals from this chapter that you can take immediate action on:

3

THE BOARDROOM TO THE CHANGING ROOM

What is our job?

What is our job, ultimately – what are we there for?

Our job is to get results out of people

It certainly isn't about getting the results ourselves – that is a weak business. A strong business is when the results are coming from others.

I remember being at a seminar once - it had nothing to do with hairdressing, so when the keynote speaker mentioned hairdressers, my ears pricked up. The seminar was specifically for small and medium sized businesses and this speaker was outlining what he felt was the fundamental problem within many small companies.

He said that if a hairdresser wanted to open up their own business, his advice would be that they should open up something like an auto exhaust fitting business!

His reasoning went like this – he said that he hadn't met many hairdressers in his life that he thought would be very good at fitting exhausts on to cars (I know – another stereotype, but probably true!)

Therefore, if they opened up an exhaust fitting service they would have to employ people who could do that job and then manage them and the business to get good results. However, he continued, of course that wouldn't happen, the hairdresser would open up a salon, and then end up working in the business - doing hair - because they can.

Don't just work in the business – work on it

We need to learn how to work on the business as well as in it, was what he was trying to say. So if our job is to get results out of people then we need to motivate people to do that. Easy!!

But it is though? – Yes! Motivation is easy

You should see some of the looks I get from my audiences when I say that – I can see people thinking to themselves "that's all very well for you to say, but you haven't met my lot."

Nevertheless, it's true though – let me explain.

If you motivate people with things that motivate them — motivation is easy

however

If you motivate people with things that don't motivate them — yep that's difficult!

It really is as simple as that

What if we had two people and one of them (let's say Samantha) was fanatical about a particular sport and had a favourite team that was notoriously difficult to get tickets for - to see play. The other person (let's call him Craig) hated that sport and anything to do with it.

It works like this: "Samantha, I need you to do something for me — it will be hard work, will take up a lot of time including some personal time and you won't get paid any extra for doing it, but I do have two tickets to go see 'X' play next week if you are interested." - I think we can all agree that Samantha will be motivated to carry out that task.

However, how would Craig react to the same thing? Negative and de-motivated of course — he hates that sport. It's so obvious, it makes you wonder why we don't see it happen all the time.

Motivate people with things that motivate them and guess what, they are motivated.

Now of course we are all different and a good leader will spend time getting to understand their team in order to know how to press all the right buttons. However there is something interesting I think, about hairdressers. I have found that throughout my career, most of the hairdressers I've ever met actually have one motivating factor, which they all share.

A fantastic hairdresser

They want to be a fantastic hairdresser — Nobody wants to hear themselves described as a 'quite good' hairdresser. I think most of us would be disappointed even, to hear someone say we were just 'good' — we want to be great, fantastic, brilliant — we want people to go away and tell others that they have an amazing hairdresser. For years we have be-moaned the hairdressers 'ego'. Why don't we start to use it instead of moaning about it?

If you want to start getting hairdressers to achieve great things and to enjoy doing it, then you have to start using the thing that motivates them the most:

Being a fantastic hairdresser!

This is my favourite quote relating to communication. If the archer misses the target it is their aim that is wrong - it has nothing to do with the target.

Well it's exactly the same with communication. Motivation depends on communication – if your team are not motivated then you are missing the target, but it is your aim that is to blame, not the target. Now stop and ask yourself how many times we blame the target for not getting the message?

From the boardroom to the changing room

Later on in the book, we will look at the importance of recognising that everybody is different and that we need to think about how to motivate individuals in different ways. But for now I want to focus in on my 'boardroom to the changing room' principle.

This principle is simply about communication – it is asking whether that what we are doing and saying, is hitting the target.

Imagine you the manager or the coach of a sports team. Let's say it's a soccer team and they play in the English Premier League.

The archer doesn't blame the target when they miss

From the boardroom to the changing room

You may be sitting in the boardroom pre-season, in a meeting that is discussing the club's goals for next season. The focus of the meeting is all about qualifying for the European Champions League next season. The financial director points out that this could be worth an extra 40-50 million in revenue plus the fact that the team's sponsor will fund the re-development of the stadium if they qualify for Europe. The FD will now pass round a spreadsheet showing how this will affect the club with an increase of 23% in ticket sales, an 18% increase in food and beverage sales and an estimated 28% increase in merchandising.

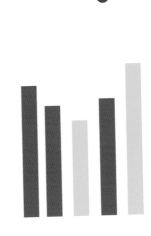

FOCUS

I think you would leave that meeting crystal clear on what your objectives are – you have to get your team into the top four in order to qualify for Europe. So, you now leave the boardroom and walk over to the changing room where the players are waiting to hear from you, as to what you think you can all achieve this season.

Now it doesn't matter if you don't know anything about soccer, or any sport in fact, but I think we all know, you wouldn't now walk into the changing room and say this:

"Ok guys, we have an exciting season ahead of us – we are going to increase the revenue at this club by over 40 million. Not only that, the sponsors are going to extend the ground which means an increase of 23% in ticket sales, an 18% increase in food and beverage sales and an estimated 28% increase in merchandising."

Of course you wouldn't – so what would you talk about?

SOCCER!

It is your job to get results out of people, to get them playing soccer so well that they get great results, which will mean that they finish in the top four of the league and qualify for Europe - so that you can now go back into the boardroom and give them what <u>they</u> wanted.

➤ The goals were exactly the same, you just communicated them differently

What I think is going wrong in many salons is that we are trying to motivate people to achieve the company's goals by using 'boardroom' language when we are in the 'changing room' with our team.

➤ The evolution of a hairdresser!

Let me tell you something else – something about the evolution of a hairdresser in the last 10-15 years;

➤ they have learnt to nod wisely

They don't have a clue what we are talking about half the time. They switch off and have learnt that they will get away quicker if they just nod wisely and pretend to agree.

The language we are using doesn't make sense and it certainly won't motivate them.

Try this – go up to a stylist and without giving any clue with your facial or body language as to whether what you are going to say is good or bad, and tell them that their colour was 32% last week.

Now watch the turmoil that will be going on in their head as they try to work out how to respond – they'll be thinking - is that good or bad? What should they do? - Look suitably embarrassed and nod wisely, or look as though they are over the moon with the news you have just given them? It's hilarious to watch because that statement on it's own doesn't mean anything. However it is the sort of thing I am hearing happen all the time.

But what if you put it across it in this way:

"You did 40 clients last week and only 7 of them walked out of the door having had colour on their hair – if you were doing a hair show tomorrow, how many models on that catwalk would have colour on their hair?"

That is a much more powerful message and it also makes sense – I would understand what you are saying to me.

It is like average client spend, or average bill if you prefer (again, we will discuss this in more detail in later chapters) but we have made it a measurement of money and productivity.

You sit them down and tell them that their average client spend is too low and that they need to do more colour, sell more products and treatments. What do they do? – They nod wisely!! They promise to try, they agree that they need to more and then get up to leave. And do you know what? Most of the time they don't give it another thought – they are just pleased to get out of there without too much pain. Meanwhile you sit there thinking - that seemed to go well. But you will notice within a couple of weeks that not much has changed.

Motivate people with things that motivate them – what motivates most hairdressers?

Being a fantastic hairdresser!

You see, 'average client spend' is a measurement of money and productivity, but only in the boardroom.

In the changing room, it is a measurement of how good a hairdresser you are

Our job is to make people look and feel fantastic – the more people you have walking out the door with colour on their hair, the correct products and having had a lovely relaxing scalp massage and hair treatment, the more people you have walking out the door looking and feeling fantastic.

Average client spend is a way of measuring how good a hairdresser you are

This must mean you are a great hairdresser – Oh and by the way, it will also mean you have a high average client spend, which means that your average client spend actually becomes a way of measuring how good a hairdresser you are... **OUCH!**

Now they will listen!!

If your team are not motivated to achieve the results you need them to, it is probably because your communication is letting you down – your aim is wrong and you are missing the target.

Establish your business goals in the boardroom and then find a way to communicate those goals in the changing room that firstly make sense and secondly are motivating enough to get people to achieve the results you need them to.

I have three favourite quotes that I always use, to explain modern leadership.

"Lead people – walk behind them"

This is where leadership has changed the most – old style leadership was from the front, with the team following you out of the trenches and on to the battlefield.

If you do that in your business today, you will be on your own in 'no mans land' whilst over a cup of tea in the trenches, the team will be remarking on how brave you are.

It is important here to re-establish something we discussed earlier in 'Balance' – this is not about soft leadership or even non-existent, this is simply about leadership coming from a different direction – literally.

Think about how a sheep dog works. They lead the sheep from one pen to another from behind, gently nudging back on track, any that wander off course. That's great leadership.

When the best leaders' work is done, the team say – we did it ourselves

I'm pretty sure that the sheep think they got there all on their own – I bet they don't have a clue how much the dog had to do with it.

This by the way is one of the reasons why women make such good leaders today – women are brilliant at getting men to do what they want without us poor guys having a clue that it was all their idea in the first place!! They also don't have the 'male ego' need to be recognised as to how clever they are for having done that.

If a man gets a woman to do something, they will probably boast about how they managed to get them to do it, whereas women will tend to keep it quiet.

You measure a great leader by what happens when they are <u>not</u> there

In other words, it is no good if it all goes wrong the moment the leader turns their back – you are a great leader if you have built a team that operates at a high level whether you are there or not.

Commitment

I will always remember a salon owner once saying to me that her team weren't committed to what she wanted to do with the salon. I replied to her by saying: "Why should they be?"

Her answer amazed me – "because they should" she said.

People won't be committed to what you want, they will be committed to what they want, and they certainly won't be committed just because you think they should be. Let's be clear about this – most people see their job as just that – a job. The few that don't, well they are no problem because their attitude means they do everything and more than you want from them. It's everybody else that drives you mad!

Commitment. That's a big word and certainly one that goes way beyond going to work to do the job you are paid to do. If you want commitment from people, you have to do much more than just expect it. The trick is to make your goals their goals. Then you have a chance. This is what leadership is all about, great communication that motivates people to want to achieve the goal they helped create.

Ok – we have finished the groundwork now.

It is important to me that you understand - everything that follows is built upon the attitudes we have been discussing in these first three chapters. Otherwise, it just won't work – it will be the same as everything else we have done in the past. Remember the fly test?

The foundations

A fantastic salon will have kept the passion, have the stability of being balanced and will take consistent action.

A fantastic salon owner understands that 50% of what will make them successful is 'the other stuff', whilst realising that to stay ahead of the game they must position themselves and their business in the outer circle of the Total Life Concept - learning, changing and being innovative and creative - all of the time.

Finally, 'from the boardroom to the changing room' - a concept based firmly upon the fly test, which is to say that if it isn't working, change something. It is simply about changing the way we communicate, motivate and lead people to success. Our job is to get results out of people, which means they have to want to achieve those results. In many cases, our communication and leadership skills are turning people off – rather than on!

If you have got all that, great. It is now time to move to the five pillars.

The boardroom to the changing room

Are you turning your team off the more you try to turn them on? The goal is the same in both rooms — but if you don't change the way you deliver it, it won't work in the changing room.

Motivation is easy

Remember — Motivation is easy if you motivate people with things that motivate them — try and motivate people with things that don't — yep that's difficult. Use the ego of the hairdresser to motivate — we all want to be 'fantastic hairdressers'!

The archer doesn't blame the target

If your message is not getting through — if it is not working — it is no good blaming them — the target — you have to look at your aim. This is why the boardroom to the changing room is so important.

Lead people - walk behind them

Times change — what used to work doesn't necessarily work now. When you lead from the front the team will sometimes just sit there and watch you — lead from behind, supporting, motivating and encouraging people to succeed.

Choose 3 goals from this chapter that you can take immediate action on:

4

THE 5 PILLARS

Ok. Let's build on those foundations then.

The 5 pillars of a successful business – any business, it doesn't make any difference. The principles I am going to discuss here apply to all.

Imagine your business supported by 5 pillars, holding it up high in the air, standing proud over all other businesses – it's a fantastic business – a fantastic salon.

It is the strength of those pillars that will take your business to the top and then most importantly, keep it there.

Of course it is possible to build your business on weak pillars, so that it looks tall and proud to anyone who is looking, however it will not withstand the ravages of time and will start to weaken and then possibly fall.

The 5 pillars that support any business are

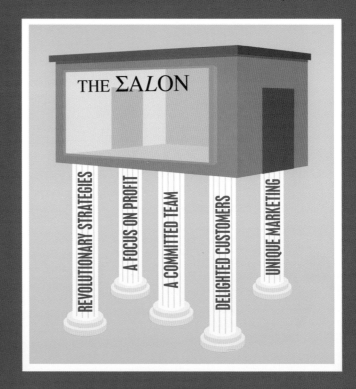

THE 5 PILLARS

The key to this though, is that all 5 pillars have to be as strong as each other. What happens if one of them is weak or non existent – your business will not be as stable. If there are two missing then it is definitely getting rocky and if three or more are weak then you are in danger of the whole thing crashing down around you.

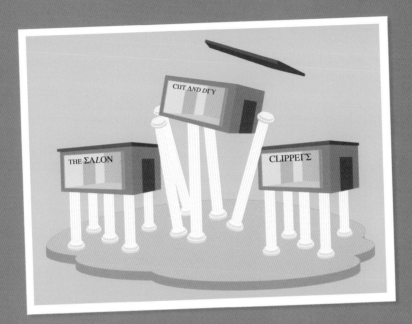

For example, look at how some businesses build themselves on just one pillar – marketing and PR. You can make that business look taller and bigger than any others out there, but it will be swaying in the wind with possible problems later on when things get tough.

Maybe you do not have the balance in your business and although it is being run with clear strategies and a strong focus on profit, the team are unhappy, which will mean that you'll not be delighting your clients. I see this often when someone from outside the industry brings in the 'hard' business principles that the salon needs, but neglects the 'soft' stuff that results in a happy team.

I personally think this is something that is happening throughout the business world in general. Although when you look at so many of the successful companies out there, they all seem to understand that it doesn't matter how good your strategy is and how well you manage the finances if you haven't got anyone willing to work for you!

Maybe we will look back and see that it all went wrong when accountants started running companies – sorry Tim! (my FD – one of the few innovative and entrepreneurial accountants I have met, which means he has the balance) Are you beginning to understand this balance thing now?

Be careful that the influence your advisors have on your business does not make it imbalanced. I have so many stories that prove this but just a couple of examples for now: There was an accountant who told a salon owner to let three stylists go, to bring down the wage bill. Luckily, she also spoke to me and I could see that there were some simple things that she could do at no cost, which would bring in enough clients to make those stylists profitable.

Then another salon owner who wanted to borrow £7,000 from his bank to invest in the Fantastic Hairdresser Ambassador Programme.

The bank refused, saying it could not see how spending that sort of money on training could be a tangible investment. The salon owner went to a different bank and got the loan.

When he started the programme, he had 6 stylists averaging 30 clients a week with an average client spend of £32. Twelve months later, he had 7 stylists averaging 35 clients a week with an average client spend of £44.

His average weekly sales had increased from 5,760 to 10,780. If you take that level of growth over just 4 weeks, a gross profit of 35% of just the growth revenue had paid off his original investment.

He then made an appointment with his previous bank. When he arrived it was clear that the original bank manager thought he was coming back to say he had made a mistake and could he move his account back again. How I wish I could have been there to see the manager's face when the salon owner showed him what had happened to his business in just a 12 month period because of the investment - that the bank manager had not felt was worthwhile.

The moral of these stories and many others I could tell you, is this: Listen to your advisors, of course. Take on board what they say, then add in the other elements to make sure you have a balance before you make your business decision. It is your business after all – you might make a wrong decision of course but that is all part of the learning/developing process.

Read some biographies and you will see how many bad decisions and mistakes people like Branson etc., have made. I myself lost over 500,000 on a bad decision (I will never bet on the horses again – only joking!) but I learnt so much from it.

Ok, the message here is simple:

It is the balance of the 5 pillars that makes your business strong. 1, 2, 3 or even 4 are not enough – you must have all 5 operating at the same level.

Revolutionary strategies

Are you strategic – do you know where you are going – specifically – where you are starting from and what you have to do get to where you are going? We must be strategic but our strategies must also be revolutionary. In other words, they must be flexible enough to cope with a rapidly changing world.

Focused on profit

Is the business so focused on sales that it forgets what the business is all about – profit. If you are not making profit what is the point? It's like buying something on e-bay and then selling it again for the same amount! What is the point?

A committed team

As we have already started to discuss, how on earth do you expect to achieve all this success without a committed team working with you?

Delighted customers

It is all about the experience that someone receives. When your clients are 'delighted', they will keep coming back for more as well as telling all their friends how fantastic you are – it's not rocket science. Customer service is not enough any more – that has become the norm.

Unique marketing

Now of course it is no good having this fantastic business if no-body knows about it. Your brand, your reputation, has to be out there for all to see. However, please, please, please, use the wonderful creativity that exists in this business – look at how many creative people you have working with you and make your marketing unique, innovative and exciting. I sometimes feel that for a creative industry we can be so un-creative in our approach to business.

Don't just serve your customers — delight them

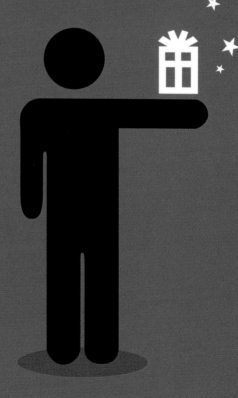

Your business development plan:

Mark yourself out of 10 for each of the five Pillars – you are not allowed to mark yourself 7 as that is the 'safe' score – it's when you are sitting on the fence. If it is looking like a 7, then you now have to make a decision – can you honestly put an 8 or is it really a 6 – make a decision!

Now commit to some action that you can take which will increase your score. If you have scored any of the pillars high – well done. However, you still need to develop your strengths. Focus on the strengths that can be developed as much as the areas that need to improve – what do you need to do to get to 20?!

Action

Revolutionary Strategies

1 2 3 4 5 6 7 8 9 10

A Focus on Profit

1 2 3 4 5 6 7 8 9 10

A Committed Team

1 2 3 4 5 6 7 8 9 10

Delighted customers

1 2 3 4 5 6 7 8 9 10

Unique marketing

1 2 3 4 5 6 7 8 9 10

Choose 3 goals from this chapter that you can take immediate action on:

5

REVOLUTIONARY STRATEGIES

Being strategic in your business means that you are ahead of yourself - working towards something and being pro-active with what needs to be done to 'get there'.

If you do not have a strategy, you will be working from day to day and most of what you have to do will be re-active.

I believe that many of the consistency problems the industry face, as previously discussed, are simply down to us not being strategic.

I was talking about this to a group of salon owners a few days before Valentine's day – I asked them who was ready for Valentine's day, what were they going to do? Give every client a red rose, or some chocolates? Had they perhaps approached a local florist and suggested some co-operative marketing, where the salon gave the florist some small gift vouchers that would slip inside the envelope to go in with the flowers, etc?

Their faces said it all – they knew that they should have done something but it would now mean running around like crazy, trying to get it done in time.

A strategic company would have had all this ready well in advance and would've saved money too. Try buying 60 red roses just a couple of days before Valentine's day. You would be paying premium price and nobody would be prepared to do a deal.

Strategy simply means having some sort of plan – a focus that identifies where you are going and a plan of how to get there. However, one of the things that many people miss, is that you have to identify where you are in the first place.

Even if you know where you are going, how can you work out how to get there if you don't know where you are starting from?

What do you need to know?

There is so much to measure in a business and in this information age, I sometimes think we have an overload of data. Be honest – you may have this whizzy computer in your salon which gives you all those reports you were so impressed with when it was demonstrated to you, but how many of those reports do you use? How many of the reports that you do use, do you actually look at?

As I always say – I am a simple man and I like things to be simple.

A client of mine wanted me to help him set up his business in such a way that he could go and live in Spain whilst his business still operated in the UK. The plan was that he would come back every 6 weeks for a few days, to deal with anything that needed his personal attention, but otherwise his management team would run the business. He had two good managers and an educator in the salon and we put a training programme in place for them.

We then set up an internet link so that he could have face-to-face meetings with his managers if needed. Finally we needed some sort of reporting system. First of all he wanted to be able to access the system in the salon for whenever he wanted to check up on things. This meant that he would have live information at the touch of a button. He could even see what the 'book' looked like - when people were taking lunch etc.

Sounds great doesn't it.

Does it??

"Why are you moving to Spain?" I asked him. He became slightly defensive as he told me that he had worked hard all his life and felt he deserved a break. He wanted a more relaxed lifestyle, to spend more time with his wife and enjoy some of the good things in life etc.

"Absolutely" I said "you do deserve it – so why on earth do you want to spoil it by worrying about the fact that the salon is not very busy one morning, or why too many people are having lunch at the same time?"

If he had access to the sort of live information he wanted, all he'd be doing is stressing himself because he was too far away to do anything about it!

This is what we ended up with:

He receives just three numbers every week – these numbers are based on the targets and budgets that had been set for the year, and had agreed benchmarks to measure against

1. Client count – how many clients the salon had done that week

2. Client spend – the average amount of money each client spent

3. Profit target - were they up or down on the profit budget that week

Keep it simple – what else did he need to know? What else do you need to know?

Nothing!

As long as the numbers are matching up to the benchmarks – "But what if they aren't?" I hear you say. Well there is a box under your front desk that has all the information you need – when you need it. It's called a computer! Instead of printing off loads of reports, (that we hardly ever look at) use the system you have, when you need it.

You have missed your client count benchmark for a couple of weeks – is it seasonal? Well you should have considered that when you created the benchmarks, so it shouldn't be. Open up the box and have a look.

Is it the amount of new clients that are down? – If so, why? Have you cut back on marketing? Have the team stopped giving out 'introduce a friend' vouchers? Has a new salon opened?

Is it repeat business? – Do you have a hole in the bucket? Is it the salon as a whole or specific individuals? Has the number of non-returning clients increased over the last 3 months – if so what has changed – have service levels slipped, is someone poaching clients to do at home etc?

Is your client visit frequency slipping? Has re-booking slowed up – is there someone new running the front desk, etc?

What if it is the client spend benchmark that you are falling short on?

Open the box!

Have your colour numbers slipped, your product sales, treatments, or have low price services increased – are people charging less than they should be? Is it the salon as a whole or specific individuals again?

Or finally, are you down on your profit target?

Where are you overspending? Was it a business decision to overspend, if so how will you recoup it? Maybe the budget was unrealistic (with either sales targets or expenditure) and it needs to be re-done, or are you just spending too much? If so - stop it!

Or, are those three numbers hitting or exceeding the benchmarks you have set? –

Then open up another bottle of Rioja!

"Let your managers to do their job" I told him "you are getting weekly figures and you will know pretty quickly if it's going wrong but otherwise sit back, take a sip of wine and relax."

So where do we start this journey?

The first things to look at are what I call the three salon drivers

Average Client count

Average Client visit

Average Client spend

If we are looking at sales, then these are the critical drivers and small changes in them can have an astonishing impact in your business.

Let's take a small/medium sized salon with a turnover of 436,800 (inc. sales tax) per year. (It doesn't matter what the numbers are, the principles I am about to go through will work on any number) Try it with your own sales in a moment.

If you prefer to look at the numbers without sales tax, then remember to take sales tax off your average bill as well.

What are the salon drivers for this business?

Average Client count	240 per week
Average Client visit	every 8 weeks
Average Client spend	35

We now have a formula that we can use

This salon has approximately 1,920 live clients on their data base (240 clients a week visiting on average every 8 weeks = 1,920 clients in total over that 8 week period) It is surprising how few clients you actually need in your bucket, to run a successful salon. As long as the bucket doesn't have a hole in it!

Sometimes people tell me that they have crazy amounts of clients on their data base 10/12/15,000 etc. I say – "Where do keep the keep the private jet?!" All those figures mean, is that you are not cleaning up your database – I am talking about 'live' clients here – people who are currently visiting you on a regular basis.

Ok, this salon is also getting about 6.5 visits a year from those clients –
52 divided by 8 (weeks in between visits) = 6.5

So, the formula is:

1,920 clients visiting 6.5 times a year spending an average of £35 each visit

$1,920 \times 6.5 \times 35 = 436,800$ - the salon's annual sales

Now let's see what happens when we play with some of these drivers:

What if we really focus on re-booking and reduce the client visit figure to 6 weeks – that is now 8.6 visits a year.

$1,920 \times 8.6 \times 35 = 577,920$

That is an increase in sales of 32%

This is a particularly good strategy for improving your salary percentage, as it will increase the amount of clients you do each week without getting any new clients.

For example, 1,920 clients coming every 6 weeks instead of 8, becomes 320 clients a week rather than 240.

Therefore, instead of eight stylists doing 30 clients a week on average, you would now have eight stylists doing 40 clients a week. And that is without any new clients!

However, you would get new clients and as long as you increase the level of experience they receive and start to 'delight' them more, you should be able to reduce the hole in your bucket and keep them too – but let's be conservative here and just add 10% to our client numbers.

$$1,920 + 192 \ (10\%) = 2,112$$

So, the new formula looks like this

$$2,112 \times 8.6 \ (6 \ weekly \ visit) \times 35 =$$

$$635,712$$

That is now an increase of 45% on our original figure

Remember that was being realistic, as just 20 new clients a week would give the salon over 1,000 new clients over the year.

If that were so, we are allowing for a client drop of just over 800 clients - meaning that in this scenario, you would still be losing 16 clients a week, every single week – that is how realistic we are being here.

Average Client Spend

Finally let's look at client spend – well I know from experience how the principles of the Fantastic Hairdresser can drive this up – we have many customers who are seeing increases in client spend of 10,15,and over 20, when they implement the secrets of the Fantastic Hairdresser.

However, I do not want anyone reading this to think that I am asking too much here, so I am only going to increase the average client spend in this case by just 5!

This is how it works – let us assume that you are starting a 2 year strategy, and that in the first twelve months you were going to focus on just 3 things – re-booking, plugging the hole in the bucket - with a better experience and delight and increasing client spend through more colour, treatments etc.

If at the end of that year, all you had accomplished was an average client visit of 6 weeks, only managed to grow your client base by 192 clients and had just achieved an increase of 5 on your average client spend - I think you would actually be quite disappointed with those figures. However, it would mean that you start the second year with:

2,112 clients visiting you 8.6 times a year and spending £40 on average each time they visit which = £726,528

That is an increase of 66%

Now do you see why I call them the salon drivers?

As I said at the beginning of this exercise, with just some small changes to these drivers you can achieve astounding results.

The first part of a revolutionary strategy is to know where you are starting from – identify your salon drivers so that you know exactly where you are starting from. The other pillars will help you to reach your destination but you need to know where you are in the first place in order to identify which pillars need to be worked on.

Profit

The second thing you need to know before you start is how profitable you are as this will be critical to the second stage of the strategy - which is where we start to identify how much profit you want and need.

SWOT

Finally at this stage, you may want to try a tool that is widely used in business. It's called a SWOT analysis.

This is a brainstorming tool, which focuses you on 4 specific areas of your business:

Your Strengths   Your Weaknesses
Your Opportunities   Your Threats

It looks like this and all you do, is brainstorm each box. When you have finished, it can be useful in helping to formulate your strategy as you would want to include in the plan; how you are going to capitalise on your strengths, improve your weaknesses, take advantage of any opportunities and guard against any threats.

Your Strengths

Your Weaknesses

Your Opportunities

Your Threats

I also use this as a personal tool, and I find it a particularly good tool with certain individuals on their one to ones'. If you do use it in this way remember it is something that should be done together, not something that you do to someone.

The fantastic salon knows where they are going

The key to the second part of building your strategy features in both of my other books. In fact, barely a day goes by without me saying this to someone (I feel like a broken record, repeating myself over and over again) but this is what I will do until people start to understand this simple truth:

How on earth will you ever get to where you are going if you don't know where you are going!

How can you work out how to get there, if you don't know where 'there' is?

Imagine you were sitting in the car and about to start a journey when one of your passengers asks "Where are we going?" You reply – "I don't know. We are just going to drive around and hopefully we will end up somewhere nice!"

It would hardly inspire confidence in your passengers would it?

That's the first level of focus – none at all!!

Some people say to me "Oh I do know where I am going - what I want. I definitely want to be more successful, maybe have more salons and I often think about an academy or something like that. Oh and I want more profit too."

This is the second level of focus and is just as bad as not having a clue where you are going – if we were back in the car again you would just be telling me "We are going north" - You still can't plan the journey and you still can't work out what you have to do to get there.

It is only when the driver knows exactly where they are going that you can get the map out and work out how to get there, how long it will take, what provisions you might need etc., etc.

Where are you going – precisely? Be specific

That is the third, and only level of focus that will get you results.

The other key to focus is again something that I seem to be saying over and over again – it is not as if anyone disagrees with me – I've yet to find anyone who disagrees with what I am about to say, but sometimes it just seems as though people ignore this critical fact of life.

Where you put your focus is where you get your results

We have all experienced this in all areas of our lives - from the huge achievements right down to simply noticing the car we are thinking about buying which turns up everywhere we look.

This is why goals work. There is nothing spooky about it. When you focus on something, you are telling your 'brain filter' that this is important to you. As it sorts through the mountains of information that enters your head every day via your senses, it will alert you to anything it finds that is relevant to your focus.

Ok. If you accept the basic fact that where you put your focus is where you get your results, then you have to accept this one too:

If you put your focus in the wrong place, you will get the wrong results

I was recently working with a salon owner who had seen really good growth in their business, but had not had the same increase in profit – in fact; she was basically breaking even after we considered her salary.

As we worked through the numbers, she kept referring to her breakeven point – she knew exactly what she had to achieve to breakeven, and she kept referring to it all the time – all of a sudden it dawned on me – what was she focused on? Breakeven - and what was she achieving? Breakeven!

I see this all the time in the salon industry – people are always telling me that they are growing, increasing their sales all the time but not achieving the profit they want.

Now stop and ask yourself where the focus is in general, in your business? I could walk into a room full of salon owners and ask them what they took last week and they would be able to tell me – however if I asked the same group what they made last week, I think we know that not many would be able to give me an answer.

We are focused on sales rather than profit....and what are we getting?

High sales and low profit

I see so many salons boasting of high sales, but then when I see the real data – the facts; there is hardly any profit – certainly not what there should be for the sales they are getting.

I love this one – it's an old one but still rings true

Turnover is vanity – profit is sanity

Ok. Let's look at where you are going – what your true destination needs to be.

How can I know what your goals are though? They are specific to you as an individual and this is a book not a one to one - I am talking to thousands of people and each and every one will want to achieve different things with their business. However there is one thing that absolutely every single one of us have to focus on in order to achieve whatever our business goals are – we have to make enough profit in order to do what we want to.

The first focus has to be your profit target – everything and I mean everything else comes from that.

You want more salons? You want to have an academy or training school? How are you going to pay for it? You want to be a creative god! Where is the money going to come from for the photo shoots, PR, models, shows etc?

I will say it again – It doesn't matter what you want to achieve – it has to start with a profitable business.

I am not being contradictive here after everything I said about passion at the beginning of the book - in fact, just the opposite. I think that it is the struggle to run a profitable business today that has sucked the passion out. It all starts with you and however team orientated you are – you are still the leader and if you lose the passion, so will they.

If your business is achieving the profitability it needs to, then you will be more relaxed - which will allow the passion to flourish. What happens to the passion in a relationship when one or other of the parties are stressed? Well is it any wonder that the same thing happens in business?

We know where we are starting from and we know where we are going, now all we have to do is work out how to get there.

This is your map, and like you would map out a long journey, you must keep it close by and continually refer to it.

There are two ways you can make your plan, but both will use the other 4 pillars to identify what action has to be taken. As you will know if you have read my other books, I am a big fan of Mind Mapping - the fantastic tool developed by Tony Buzan.

Objective mapping

I have developed something called objective mapping from this, which is a tool that I use to break down every goal I set, into smaller manageable chunks. This is especially important as I always advocate that you set yourself spectacularly un-realistic goals.

Where you put your focus is where you get your results remember – so if you want average, then set average goals, but if you want spectacular and amazing, then you had better start setting spectacular and amazing goals.

This is all very well of course until you stop and ask yourself - how on earth are you going to do that? But this is where a tool like objective mapping works as it takes even the most ridiculous goals and breaks them down into small, easily achievable chunks.

You start by putting your focus in the centre – let's say that you have decided on a number that you want to achieve as an annual sales target which will also be giving you X profit.

Using positive language (much more important than you might think) it might read like this:

Monday 16th May 2010   **The Daily Mirage**

IT'S 2010 AND BIG AL'S HAIR SHOP IS TAKING 2 MILLION PER ANNUM AND MAKING 20% NET PROFIT

Lorem ipsum dolor sit amet, consectetur adipisicing elit, sed do eiusmod tempor incididunt ut labore et dolore magna aliqua. Ut enim ad minim veniam, quis nostrud exercitation ullamco laboris nisi ut aliquip ex ea commodo

SALON OF THE YEAR!

What I mean by positive language is that I am making sure there is no suggestion of not achieving it in the words that I am using. I am assuming it is going to happen – once again, this is not something weird & wacky – it is based upon science and the fact that our brain has a filter that we are feeding all this stuff into. However you have to be precise, otherwise the results you get might not be what you wanted.

Now draw in five key branches – label 4 of them with the 4 remaining pillars, whilst adding 'personal development' to the 5th one. This is where you identify anything you need to change, improve or develop in yourself.

Some of these will come out in your swot analysis, others will just become clear as you develop the plan. And of course, your own self-knowledge is enough to add in things that you know you will have to work on yourself, such as time management, self-discipline, consistency etc.

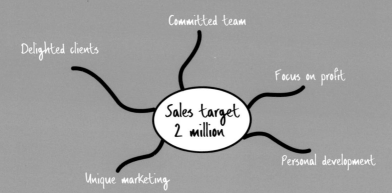

Finally, you start to map out the action that needs to be taken in each of these areas in order for you to achieve your focus in the centre. Each of those will probably break down and down, leaving you with lots of small things around the edge of the map for you to take action on.

As you start taking action on more of those things, you will be getting closer and closer to the centre of the map, closer to achieving your focus.

I suggest that you do this exercise on a piece of flip chart paper but using normal sized writing so that you can fit everything on. Do use different colours though; it makes it much more fun as well as more stimulating for the eye and the brain when you look at it.

As I have said this is my favoured way of planning. However if you do not like mapping then you can do it the old way like this:

	Quarter 1	Quarter 2	Quarter 3	Quarter 4
Focus on profit				
Committed team				
Delighted clients				
Unique marketing				
Personal development				

The Fantastic Salon knows where they are

Where are you starting from? You can't work out your route if you don't know. Use a swot analysis and the 3 salon drivers – client count, client visit and client spend. What needs to change to make you more profit?

The Fantastic Salon knows where they are going

If you don't know where you are going – how on earth are you ever going to get there? You must have a specific focus that stretches you to achieve your dreams. Where you put your focus is where you get your results!

The Fantastic Salon knows what they have to do to get there

Now make your map – you know where you are – you know where you are going – all you need now is to know how to get there. Use an objective map to turn even the biggest goals into manageable steps.

Choose 3 goals from this chapter that you can take immediate action on:

6 The Fantastic IS FOCUSED

CHAPTER 6   CHAPTER 6   CHAPTER 6   CHAPTER 6   CHAPTER 6   CHAPTER 6   CHAP

The Bank Of Fantastic

Salon
on

Profit

6

The golden rule of money

Many years ago when I was starting my first business, a family friend who had been very successful in business and was now a multi millionaire, asked me if I would like some advice.

"Of course" I said, "you have done it, I would be foolish not to listen to you."

He then proceeded to give me the most patronising advice that I could imagine.

Of course I was far too polite to tell him: "I'm not daft, everybody knows that!" - I just nodded wisely.

However after 20 years of running my own companies, of helping other people run theirs, of managing my own personal finances, my childrens' and friends' money, I now know that the advice was far from patronising. It looks it at first sight, but you must stop and ask yourself if this is how you deal with money both in business and personally.

So what was the advice?…

"To be successful in business," he said, "you must understand money, and the golden rule of money is to make sure more comes in than goes out."

Now I'm sure you can understand why I thought; yeah – tell me something I don't know. But of course so many individuals and companies just don't seem to understand how critical this basic rule is.

More has to come in than goes out – if it does – you are in business – if it doesn't – you're not!

Hamster management

I am going to simplify things here, but essentially this is how money works, whether in business or life - it is the same.

To keep things simple, let's think about it a week at a time. Now it obviously doesn't work as cleanly as this, but this is just a model to explain things.

Week one

Money comes in, but you have to use that money to make some more next week – if you don't pay the wages, nobody will come to work next week, if you don't buy the stock you can't wash anyone's hair, if you don't pay the rent the landlord won't let you in, etc

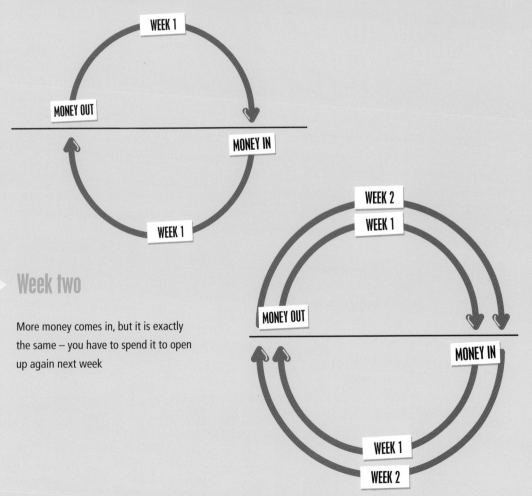

Week two

More money comes in, but it is exactly the same – you have to spend it to open up again next week

Week three - More money comes in but….. **Week four** - the same   **Week five** – and again

And so on, and on, and on….

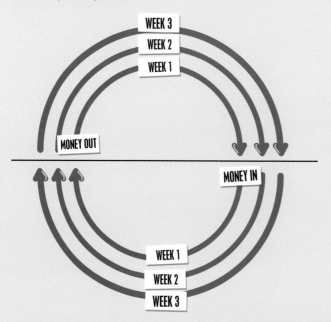

I call this hamster management – do you understand why? Have you ever seen the hamster inside the wheel working so hard to keep the wheel turning. All that effort - to go nowhere! Now do you understand?

You see, if that wheel is turning but there is no profit coming out each time it goes around – what is the point? And if the profit it is making is really your salary, then you are going through the whole process of running a salon, all that stress and responsibility – basically, just to give yourself a job.

Move back from the open window please!!

What is your business?

I often find that some people do not understand what their business actually is. They think that the hamster's wheel is their business. That is not your business, it is a process.

A process that you go through in order to make money – profit.

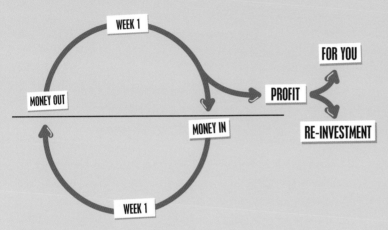

That's your business

Once again, let me remind you that I am not saying it is all about money, in fact, those that know me well, will testify that I am not at all motivated by money – however I need it to do things that do motivate me.

I did not go into business initially to make money, I went into business for freedom – but you know what, if I wasn't making any money, I wouldn't get the type of freedom I want.

Well if you haven't got this message yet – I give up – where's that window!!

Ok. Let's just remind ourselves of the critical fact – where you put your focus is where you get your results.

So let's start putting our focus on profit

In this chapter, I am going to show you how to set targets for your salon that include the profit you both need and want to make. The figures you work with here should not include sales tax.

I am also assuming that you separate out retail sales from service sales (if you don't – you should) as the percentage of retail stock cost to sales price is very different to the benchmarks you would be using in services.

The same applies to beauty if you offer this service, as once again the percentages are different to what I will be talking about. However the principles still apply so you can work out what the targets are for beauty in the same way, just with different numbers.

You can add them all together later if you wish to have an overall salon target, but you would have to work them out separately first.

Finally, the numbers I will use here are based upon average benchmarks in the UK – it doesn't matter if the benchmarks in your country are different as the numbers I am using are only to demonstrate the formula – you would have to put your own 'actual' figures in anyway.

This is how your business breaks down:

Firstly, we have salaries and stock. These are always expressed as a percentage because they are what is known as variable costs – they change in line with your sales. The more sales you take - the higher your salary bill will be, the more business you do - the more stock you would have to buy, and vice versa.

Then whatever is left is known as gross profit. The way I always describe gross profit is; if you had a salon on the beach, once you had paid the team, and bought any stock you needed, whatever is left would be your profit.

However, unfortunately you are probably not on the beach but in a salon elsewhere - which means that you have to use that gross profit to pay all your other bills - rent, utilities, marketing, training, refreshments etc.

Anything left after all that is called net profit – and that is yours, after you have given your donation to your government's piggy bank of course!

Therefore, these are the numbers you need:

Annual salary as a percentage of 'service' sales

This should include everybody who is involved in providing the service in the salon (yes that does mean front desk and assistants as well as stylists, and if you are productive on the floor it must include you too) as well as all employment taxes.

Team members who work in the office and cleaners etc., as well as yourself - if you do not do clients, are entered into 'other costs' later. If you spend some days in a management capacity and some as a stylist, then apportion it accordingly.

Annual 'service' stock purchases as a percentage of 'service' sales

Your bookkeeper or accountant should be able to tell you what both of these figures are.

Let's say that your salaries come out at 50% and your stock purchases at 10%, then that leaves 40% gross profit

Salaries 50% + Stock 10% = 60%
So Gross profit = 40%

All other costs for the year

Now you need to do your budget – list out all the other costs involved in running your business. To determine your budget for next year, you should be able to use historical information for most of the headings – for example, you should know what your rent will be, your utility bills and so on. However, there are three headings that may not have any relevance to what happened last year.

Rent
Rates
Marketing
Training
Refreshments
Concessions

120,000

These are marketing, training, and maintenance. Decide on how much you are going to spend in these areas next year – for example you may need to get a lot of new clients, in which case you will need to budget for an increased spend in marketing, or maybe you have some work to do in the salon which needs doing this year.

Add it all up and you have an amount of money that you are budgeting to spend next year on all other costs.

For the purpose of this exercise we will say that all other costs for the year, total 120,000.

The formula

Ok, we are ready to go now.

To explain how the formula works we are going to start with a breakeven target, but then we will be able to use the same formula to build in our profit target.

What don't we know yet? – We don't know what the sales target has to be in order to pay all the bills.

What do we know? – We know that whatever that target is, 50% will go to pay the wages, 10% to buy the stock, leaving me 40% to pay the bills which all add up to 120,000.

Of course is does not work like this but for the purpose of this exercise, just imagine that you paid all your bills at the end of the year – after you had paid your wages and stock, you would need 120,000 left in the bank to pay all the other bills.

So, what we do know is that whatever our target is, 40% of it (what is left after salaries 50%, and stock 10%) needs to be 120,000 in order to pay all those other bills.

Therefore all I have to do is work out what 120,000 is 40% of, and that will be my target.

Get out your calculator and do this;

Enter 120,000, press the divide button and now enter 40, press the times button and enter 100 – what you see on the screen is the breakeven target for this salon. You should see 300,000.

The formula is:

total other costs divided by the gross profit figure x 100

telling you what 100% is – your target. By the way it doesn't matter if you don't get the math, all you need to do is press the right buttons on the calculator – or go to our website www.fantastichairdresser.com and meet 'the calculators' in our academy - our on-line learning site. These will work it all out for you in seconds.

Profit

Ok, now you understand the formula, all we have to do is build in the profit that you need and want.

What do I mean by need and want? Well I often find that even if a salon is profitable, it is not making enough to satisfy both the needs and the wants of the owners of the business.

Simply put –

the profit you need is how much you need for re-investment into the company to achieve your goals and the profit you want is exactly that, what you want for yourself.

Are you making enough profit to do both those things because you do need to. In the old days, profit went solely to the 'wants'. I always used to say that hairdressers wear and drive their profit!

However, in more recent times this has turned completely on its head. Most companies understand the slow suicide of not re-investing in the business, but now are not taking anything for themselves.

In the first scenario, it is quite clear that the business will suffer, but so will it in the second instance – once the salon owner is frustrated and fed up, then the whole business will suffer.

Do you ever have 'the sit on the edge of the bed talk'?

This is where you sit on the edge of the bed, on your own and say to yourself "what's the point?!" etc. Now do you understand where I'm coming from?

Profit must do two things, not one – there must be enough to re-invest in the business as well as enough to make you feel that it is all worth it.

What profit do you need and what profit do you want?

So finally, how do we use the formula to set targets for profit? This is how it works so far:

Let's say we want 10% profit, where in the pie is that?

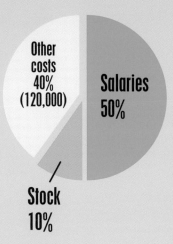

You can't just add 10% on to the breakeven – this is a common mistake that people make, ending up with the wrong targets. That won't take into account the fact that however much money you put in the till, 60% (in our example) will always come back out again for salaries and stock.

We have to make it all come from the same pie – the bills, the salaries, the stock and the 10% profit you want.

Well we want 10% profit. Can we take it off the salaries? I don't think that will go down well, what about not buying any stock – obviously not. There is only one place it can come from – we have to change the 40% that we had to pay our costs - to 30%. That now allows for 10% net profit for you!

So now we do the formula again but this time using 30 instead of 40

120,000 divided by 30 x 100 = 400,000

That is the target for this salon to make 10% profit – the first thing you should notice is that it is considerably more than if we had just added 10% to our original break even of 300,000.

What if you want 15% profit – then do the sum with 25 this time instead of 30.

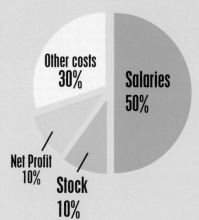

20% profit – there is only 20 left now to pay the bills, so do the sum with 20 to find out the target.

It's that simple – you now have an annual target based upon your expenditure budgets which includes a level of profit that you have decided is right for yourself and your business.

Just having a target will not achieve anything for you unfortunately – if only it were that easy.

Yes, it's true that you have improved the odds dramatically of achieving what you need to, simply because you now know what it is that you need to achieve.

However, you still have to take the action needed to achieve it, and perhaps most importantly of all you have to consistently measure where you are.

If we continue with the analogy of the journey that we have been using, then you need to keep one eye on the road signs to make sure you are going in the right direction, otherwise one wrong turn could spell disaster.

The road signs that you will be using are the ones that we discussed in chapter 5. As we agreed earlier, these three numbers actually give you all the information you need.

The first thing you have to do is break them down into weekly targets that will make sense to the team – how you use these targets will be discussed in

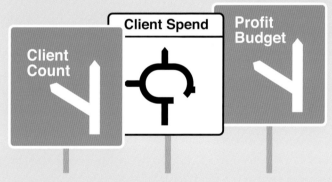

chapter 7, but for now let's just find out what they are.

Unless you have really educated your team otherwise, I feel that it is important to add sales tax onto the target now, so that it makes sense in the real world of the 'changing room'.

Remember it is all about communication and making sure your team understand the information you give them. Most people – probably even yourself, look at what goes in the till. We know that sales tax has to be deducted, but we still refer to the number as a gross figure, including tax.

Again, I ask you what would happen if I quizzed a room full of salon owners as to how much they took last week – how many would give me a net figure?

Let's take the salon we used earlier and set them a target to achieve 15% net profit.

120,000   divided by   25   x   100

(Other costs)   (25 being what is left of the original gross profit (40%) to pay the bills after allocating 15% for net profit)

That gives us a target of 480,000, giving us 240,000 to pay the wages (50%), 48,000 to spend on stock (10%) plus the 120,000 that is in our budget for all the other costs, leaving us with a net profit before tax, of 72,000, which is 15%.

So, it works. The amount of money needed to pay the salaries has increased, which means if extra team members were needed to achieve the target, the funds are there.

There is enough in the pot to buy the extra stock that is needed to service the increase in business (this is why these figures are always shown as a percentage) and as long as the 'other costs' budget is kept to, the profit will be there.

Target breakdown — the salon success standard

Step 1

Add on sales tax – I am going to use 17.5% the UK vat rate.
The target is now 564,000.

Step 2

Divide this number by 52 – some of you may be used to dividing this by 40 something to allow for holidays etc. This would be correct if it were an individual stylist, but your salon is open 52 weeks of the year and we need to find out what the average weekly take needs to be in order for you to hit your target.

The weekly target including sales tax (what you have to put in the till) is now 10,846.

Step 3

Decide on how many clients you can sensibly accommodate each week in the salon – bear in mind four factors; opening times, amount of stylists, space/chairs and service standards.

Let's say that this salon has 8 stylists that can comfortably do 40 clients a week. Now this is where you have to make an adjustment to take into account holidays, nominal sickness and un-booked time etc., over the year (nobody is going to be fully booked every day of the year, even your busiest stylist will have people cancelling or not turning up)

As a rule of thumb I normally deduct between 10 -15% depending on your holiday entitlement and bank holidays etc.

So let's say that in this case we are going to knock 5 clients off that figure to make it realistic over the year – 8 stylists doing 35 clients a week.

This gives us a salon - client count target of 280.

Step 4

Now divide your weekly sales target by the client count target to find out the average client spend target.

10,846 divided by 280 = 38.73 – let's call it 40.

This salon now has what I call 'the salon success standard' which is expressed as weekly client count @ average client spend

280@40

That's it. As long as the salon is achieving that benchmark, they will achieve their target.

Sales target inc. tax = 564,000

% by 52 weeks = 10,846

8 stylists @ 35 clients per week = 280

10,846 / 280 = 40 average client spend

To achieve weekly sales of 10,846 I need 280 clients per week spending an average of 40

You can now make seasonal adjustments to that figure if you wish, as well as break it down further to individual stylists, giving them their own stylist success standard. Make sure you check that it all still adds up to the annual figure though - after you have made those adjustments. Some people actually set the weekly and individual stylist targets so that they add up to more than is needed, giving them some leeway to allow for things not always going to plan.

You now have a weekly focus for the salon as well as individual stylists, that is based upon the profit you want to make over the year.

In 'the calculators' I mentioned earlier – that are in our on-line academy, you can do an exercise with an individual stylist by asking them how much they want to earn. By inputting their average wage as a percentage of what they take, you can show them how many clients they have to do a week and at what average client spend, in order to earn their required salary. It's great!

PROFIT BUDGET

Finally, we just have to make sure that the profit is there at the end of the year. It is no good hitting your targets all year, to find that you have overspent and that there is still no profit left.

What if our salon didn't watch what went out as much as they watched what came in and they overspent on their other costs by just 10% - that's an extra 12,000 - they didn't control the salary percentage which slipped to 54% instead of 50% and they also overspent on stock letting the budget of 10% slip to 13%.

Nothing major – it's not like they have gone mad, but look what happens:

Let's assume that they hit their sales target of 480,000

They will now have spent 259,200 on salaries, instead of the 240,000 it was meant to be

62,400 instead of 48,000 on stock purchases

And their fixed costs are now 132,000 instead of 120,000 because they over spent by 10%

That all adds up to 453,600 leaving a net profit of 26,400 instead of 72,000!!

You have just lost 45,600 profit

In fact to make the 72,000 profit you were going to, you would now have to achieve sales of 618,000 - an extra 2,653 per week!!!

Hopefully now you can understand why it sometimes seems as though you are busier than ever, putting loads of money in the till, but still not making the profit you want to.

If all you are looking at is what comes in, then it will be leaking out at the other end. If this is you, just think about how much profit (your money) you have lost over the years, simply because you were watching what comes in and not what goes out.

Move back from that open window - there is still work to be done here!!

Do you remember the 'patronising' advice I was given 20 years ago when I started out in business – the golden rule of money:

More has to come in than goes out

If this is relevant to you – I hope I have frightened you enough to get control of it, otherwise you really are on that hamster wheel, working really hard, dealing with all that stress – going nowhere.

Use your profit budget

Just having a profit budget won't help your business to make profit, but using one will.

It's very simple – list all the headings of all your costs, and then draw in 3 columns,

Budget	Actual	+/-

Break the annual budget down into a monthly budget, and then fill in the actual (what you actually spent) column each month. Now compare it to the budget (what you were supposed to spend) column, and write the difference in the final (+/-) column.

If you have spent more than you should, enter it as a minus figure as it means that you are missing that amount of money now from the plan - you have spent it, it's gone. If you spent less than you were going to, enter it as a plus figure, as you now have more money than you expected.

Finally total up the plusses and minuses and enter the result in the 'total' box at the bottom of the column. Now bring forward your running total from last month in the b/f (bought forward) box, add the two together and you have a new running total in the c/f (carry forward) box.

BUDGET SHEET			MAY
ITEM	**BUDGET**	**ACTUAL**	**+/-**
Sales	40,000	40,000	
Wages %	20,000	22,000	- 2000
Stock %	4,000	4,000	
Rent	3,000	3,000	
Rates	500	500	
Electric	100	100	
Refreshments	500	300	+ 200
marketing	1,500	2000	+ 500
training	2,000	1000	+ 1000
	300	500	- 200
		TOTAL	- 500
		brought forward	+ 1,700
		carry forward	+ 1,200

This figure will go up and down as you will sometimes be over budget and at other times, under budget. Maybe you decide to spend more than you were going to this month on marketing, or a new product – that's ok, budgets shouldn't restrict your business. However, the difference now is that you know you have gone over budget – you have made a business decision to go over budget - as long as you realise that you will have to get it back in line somehow in the future.

If the running total is showing a trend of consistently getting worse though, it will be for one of two reasons and you will have to take action quickly.

Either you are spending more than you should be – answer – stop it!

Or your budget is wrong – the original expenditure targets, percentages or sales targets were not realistic – answer – start again – do another budget

Go right back to the beginning. Set a new salary percentage, stock percentage and total other costs figure. Make a decision on how much profit you want - maybe this is the building year and you won't make as much. Whatever, make the changes as needed and then use the formula again.

You will have a new sales target. Break it down and you will have a new salon success standard and a new budget.

Off you go again.

With this system there should be no surprises – you will know exactly where you are and what is going on at any time with just three numbers:

Client count, Client spend, Running +/- budget total

If you are hitting all three numbers – whoopee!

If not, take appropriate action which will probably come from the following three chapters where we look at the last three pillars - a committed team, delighted customers, and unique marketing. Have fun!

The Fantastic Salon understands how money works

Understand the difference between the process and the result – the general running of the business, bringing money in and then spending it to bring in more is just a process – the result of that process is profit. What is the point of going through the process without the result?

The Fantastic Salon is focused on profit

Where you put your focus is where you get your results – where is your financial focus – are you solely focused on sales – what you put in the till? Or are you focused on profit – watching what goes out as keenly as you watch what comes in?

The Fantastic Salon knows what is going on

Set your annual target, break down into measurable benchmarks – client count and client spend. Then create a profit budget so that you know exactly what is going out as well. Now use these benchmarks consistently so that you know exactly what is going on and you can take any action needed quickly.

Choose 3 goals from this chapter that you can take immediate action on:

THE FANTASTIC SALON HAS A COMMITTED TEAM

All we have to do now is get the team to commit to the targets and goals that we have set – easy!!

What is a team?

I want to start by understanding the fundamental principle of what makes a committed team rather than a nice group of people who just happen to work in the same place.

This is the definition of a team

A team is a group of individuals who are working together... to achieve a common goal

And here is the definition of a group – the opposite to a team

A group is a group of individuals who are working together...

That's it – there is nothing more – a group is a group of people who are working together.

So the only difference between a group and a committed team is that in a team, those same people are now working together to achieve something – sound familiar?

If you don't know where you are going…

Think about it, when do your team operate at their best? I bet it's when there is something to focus on. For example, the day that you think is going to be a nightmare: It's a really busy day, columns are full and people are off sick – Well, it turns out to be a great day because everyone pulls together and works as a **TEAM** - to get through the day.

Well we have a goal, but it is **our** goal at the moment - not the team's goal. What we have to do now is communicate to the team in such a way that our goal becomes their goal.

From the boardroom to the changing room

The salon focus

What we are going to do here is get the team to commit to a goal that they have been a part of creating, which will still however link back to the goals that you set earlier.

Step 1

Arrange a team meeting and start the meeting by asking everyone to write down what they love about their job – why do they come to work every day? Agree that obviously one of the reasons is because we get paid, but you get paid to do any job, so why do we do this one? (This bit is important as it stops the cynic from de-railing you with the smug comment that; the only reason they come to work is because they get paid to)

This is just a bit of preparation that will make sure their focus is on what they like about their job before you move to the next stage.

Step 2

Introduce the concept of; "if you don't know where you are going – how on earth do you expect to get there?" Then ask them how they want their salon to be perceived – how do they want people to think of it – do they care if no-one has a clue who or where they are, or do they want the salon to be recognised? Do they want people to say "wow" when they tell them where they work or; "where's that?"

You know what they will say — of course they will want people to say wow. They want the salon to be recognised.

Step 3

Ask them what they want the salon to be recognised as.

You will get all sorts of answers but they will all be positive. And I guarantee, someone will say "the best" or something like that. As soon as someone says that, grab the words out of the air and agree - this is what we all want.

We want to be recognised as the best!

Ok, so now stop and think about this. Who is going to disagree? Can you imagine one of your team interrupting with; "I don't think we want to be the best." - Of course they wouldn't say that.

Step 4

Best at what though? Now generate a discussion about what makes a salon the best – you will find that they all agree, it is not just about hair – you could bring in the **50% principle** here.

Finally get agreement from them that our job is simply...

To make people look and feel fantastic

Step 5

Now ask them how we will measure this – **how will we know we are the best?**

Well surely the best salon in town is the one that has the most people walking around out there – **looking and feeling fantastic.** Once again, nobody can dispute this.

Point out that there are two measurements of a fantastic salon –

You measure what walks in and you measure what walks out.

What walks in – client count – if we are doing a great job we will have a high amount of people coming through the door every day. The more consistent we are, the more we delight people - the more they will return to us, as well as recommending friends to come in as well. Therefore, a high client count must mean we are doing **something right.**

What walks out - this is where we really start to measure the experience the client has had in your salon – do they look and feel fantastic when they leave the salon?

Ask your team if they feel they have really made someone look and feel fantastic with just a good haircut – ask them here:

How many models would they would put on the catwalk without colour on their hair – answer – none!

Colour is like make-up for the hair – a good haircut can get away without colour on it in the same way that a pretty girl doesn't have to wear make up but if you take that girl and use makeup well, you can turn her from pretty into gorgeous - it's the same with hair.

Are we fantastic hairdressers if the look we have created in the salon cannot be re-created at home because the client does not have the correct products in their bathroom?

And if we want to make them feel fantastic as well, what is one of the best ways to do that in a modern salon –

A gorgeous scalp massage and hair treatment

– they love it!

So if we want to be recognised as the best, we have to have loads of people walking out of the door looking and feeling fantastic - which means we have to have loads of people walking out of the door with colour, the correct products and having had a lovely treatment and scalp massage whilst in the salon.

The result of all this must be an increase in your average client spend

A high average client spend must mean that we are sending more people out of the door looking and feeling fantastic and **a high client count** must mean that they are enjoying the experience and coming back for more.

So the way to measure if we are one of the best salons around, is simply by;

how many clients we do @ a high average client spend

Ok. Do you understand what we have done here – it is the boardroom to the changing room principle – we have taken the goal we want to achieve from the boardroom and turned it into something that they want to do.

Now introduce your targets in the way I have shown you – 200 @ £60 for example.

Finally close the meeting by asking them if they understand and agree with the goal – that the team wants to be recognised as the best salon in the town/country/world whatever, and that the way that will be measured is with the salon success standard.

Assuming that they say yes, you will now have a level of commitment to the goals that you want to achieve.

Individual focus

Finally, use that agreement to focus the individuals in the team – almost any individual behaviour that needs to be developed can be linked to the team goal.

Poor timekeeping - ask the individual concerned; "how can we be the best salon, when you are arriving after your clients?"

Poor appearance, low client spend, low client numbers, poor service standards, bad attitude, conflict, hangover etc. I think you will find that anything you ever need to discuss with a team member will always link back to the overall team goal.

With this in mind, I want to spend a bit of time looking at some of the leadership problems that I see in the modern day workplace.

I want to take you back to some of the things that I said in chapter one, about balance - particularly when I was talking about leadership. I mentioned that I feel sometimes we have lost the balance in our leadership style and become so 'people and team orientated' that some members of the team start to take advantage of this - feeling that they are indispensable to the team and that you would never get rid of them.

These characters can seriously affect the harmony within the team as well undermine all the work you are doing here to get the team focused. You know who I am talking about. If you are lucky enough not to have any of these characters currently, I would be prepared to bet a lot of money that you have had in the past.

We need to start managing these people

However, part of the problem is that sometimes there is nothing to manage. If there is no goal and no structure in place to achieve that goal, all you are doing is managing the day-to-day crap – fire fighting, nagging etc.

When there is an agreed team goal, with agreed procedures and measurements in place, you have something to manage and if those individuals we are talking about are not pulling their weight, you can now take action.

The first thing you have to do though is to commit to it all yourself – are you serious about changing your business, growing it and moving it forward?

If the answer is yes, then you may have to start bringing more balance into your leadership style and toughening up on the things that matter.

I feel that sometimes the whole team message, 'empowerment' etc., has been misunderstood as; soft and cuddly, don't upset anybody, they might leave - to the point where I find many managers and owners now border on un-assertive and that can't be right.

There are three types of behaviour when you look at assertiveness

Assertive   Un-assertive   Aggressive

It seems as though many people miss this and think there are only the two: **Un-assertive and aggressive – mistakenly believing that aggressive is assertive!**

When true 'assertive' behaviour is missing from the mix, the only alternative to being aggressive is un-assertive. Not many people like to be aggressive so they end up being un-assertive - not realising that there is a third option.

Assertive is where the balance is. The following statement is about the attitude of mind that you need to have. (I am not suggesting you to say it like this – I am just pointing out where your mind should be)

"I am a nice person; I respect you, and believe in you. I want you to be successful and value you as a member of the team. I am understanding of you and do not judge you; I know that you will make mistakes and learn from them, as do I. However, this is the team goal – the reason why we all come into work every day and your behaviour is not currently in line with that goal. So therefore we need to find a way to change it. I am here to help you change and will give you all the training, support and motivation you need to make those changes. However it is ultimately your responsibility and if you don't take that responsibility then you are not going to be working here for long."

This is known as;

The loose/tight paradox

The 'looser' (team orientated etc.) your management style is, the tighter it has to be, otherwise it will just get out of control.

I believe that this is critical, as I see it happening everywhere - socially as well as in business!

Please understand –

I am not calling for a return to the old ways, just a return to some balanced ways.

I am sure some of you are agreeing with me whilst also saying, "but, it's not as easy as that Alan." Well, no-one said it was easy – if it were easy, everybody would be doing it.

However, I guess that what you are talking about is legislation and the fact that your hands are often tied by the action that you <u>can't</u> take as an employer.

Well I do understand – I am an employer too, but I think a lot of it is down to how we use the legislation that is there. For example let's look at the procedure for getting rid of people. Now I know that it is different in certain countries, but the basic premise is that you have to give some sort of verbal warning, followed by a legislated amount of written warnings before you can dismiss someone.

Try looking at this procedure differently –

Instead of viewing it as a procedure for getting rid of people, see it as a procedure for keeping people.

If you see it that way, you will use it sooner, rather than waiting till everything is lost and then deciding to start the procedure for getting rid of them.

Imagine you work for me and we've had many informal discussions about something – let's say it's time keeping.

Nothing seems to be changing. It's as if you are not taking me seriously - that you don't seem to realise the importance of what I am saying. You are in danger of starting to become someone I don't want working here -

it's time to try and save you – I am going to use the procedure for keeping people!

Next time we have to talk about your time keeping I am going to make it a formal verbal warning – imagine your shock – I think you would start taking me seriously now.

Now what is going to happen – well, one of three things:

You will either say stuff your job if that is how it's going to be, I'm leaving. - Not the result I wanted but at least I have found out early on that you are not committed to what we are doing here.

Or, you will carry on working here, but still not making the changes you need to. Well the procedure has started now and if necessary I will have to carry it through to completion. - Again not what we want but of course it could happen.

Or maybe at some stage of the procedure it becomes a wake up call for you as you realise that this is important and you start to change your behaviour. Hooray! – We have saved you!!

Recruitment

I suppose if I am telling you that in your quest towards being a fantastic salon there may be some casualties, then I guess we had better look at how we keep the team strong with a good recruitment policy.

There are two things to focus on here;

the balance of the team and your target market for recruiting new team members.

A balanced team

There's that word again. But the fact is, a good team is a balanced team. Look at any sports team and you will understand this.

When you are recruiting you must always have one eye on the balance of the team. You have an opportunity here to improve the balance within your team – don't just automatically replace what you have lost.

There are two types of balance that you need to consider, 'function' – that's the easy one – what people actually do, and 'role' – the roles that people play in the team.

'Role' can often have nothing to do with 'function' – the person running your front desk may be one of the more creative people in the team. Their function is front desk management, their role is creative – a good team needs lots of different roles – you need passionate people, creative people of course but you also need 'doers', organisers, realists, humorists, experience, naivety, superstars, as well as dependable plodders etc.

If you have too many of one type, your team will never operate as well as it could do.

The creative person needs the balance of the realist.

The humorist will stop the passionate people taking themselves too seriously; the experienced person will see things differently through the eyes of naivety; the organiser needs a doer to take the action and whilst a team full of superstars will keep you awake at night, a team full of dependable plodders will send you to sleep by day – a good team is a mix of all these and more.

Take a look at the balance of your team and you might see where some of your troubles are. Of course the problem you have is that if you do identify any in-balances, you can't just get rid of the ones that you have too many of and go buy some new models – if only it were that easy. No unfortunately this is a long term strategy based around training. First of all, identify what strengths people have outside of their function and start to develop them – it will bear fruit later I promise. The second thing that you can do, is when you need to recruit new people into the team, keep in mind what you need to improve - the balance of roles, not just function.

Your target market

How big is your target market for recruiting new team members? I am always hearing that there are no stylists out there, stories of people running adverts and getting no response etc.

No stylists out there?

There are loads of stylists out there. What people mean when they say that, is that there are no stylists within their catchment area that are actively looking for a job — the week that they put their advert in the paper!

Now that's a narrow target market — no wonder it's tough.

What is the target market then? Every stylist in the world! Ok, I am being a bit dramatic but are there not hairdressers from all around the world, working in salons in your country? - Of course there are. Let's get closer to home though. Are there stylist from different parts of the country working in salons miles away from home — yes again. Finally, you have worked with people who are prepared to travel a long distance to do the job they really want to, haven't you?

First of all don't limit yourself to the local market. Find some good reasons why someone might want to work where you are situated — for example, a small town salon can offer a less stressful and lower cost of living to a big city stylist who is getting fed up with the rat race. Now target some areas that you think might be worthwhile for you.

Of course the simplest way nowadays to appeal to a bigger market, even a global market - is through the internet. Are you using your website to actively recruit? I don't just mean having a number to call if someone is interested in working with you, I mean really getting across the message that you have something to offer.

You have to sell to prospective team members as much as you have to sell to your clients.

Use some of the specialised internet employment sites such as **www.hair-recruitment.com etc.**

Secondly, if you only market for team members when you need them you are limiting the market to a small time frame – adopt an ongoing recruitment policy all year round. No I haven't gone mad, this is recruitment not employment, I am not saying that you should employ all year round, just go through the recruitment process.

A consistent message out there –

that you are always looking to meet forward thinking people, who are willing to learn and work hard as part of a focused and energetic team in return for great money and career opportunities.

An invitation to then contact you for more information about 'how we do things here and find out when we are next employing people' will surely start to give you a short list of people who are waiting for an opportunity to work with you.

Use your own words but hopefully you get the point. Take a look at your recruitment policy. Is it geared up for ongoing recruitment and for when you are employing people and are you bearing in mind the importance of a balanced team?

The fantastic salon's team are excited about what they do

The team know where they are going now, but of course it is not as easy as that. It's now up to you to motivate them to keep focused.

As we have already discussed, consistency is the key here – you have to use the salon focus all the time to make sure that everybody keeps it in the front of their mind.

I hope that you are beginning to understand this whole 'boardroom to changing room' principle – if we want to motivate and excite the team to achieve the results we need them to - we must use things that motivate them. So far, we have focused on the fact that most of your team are motivated by being a fantastic hairdresser, which is why the exercise we just did will work.

The more you move average client spend away from how much money they are taking, towards it being just a number - a result of them simply doing their job properly, the more positively the team will see it. Have you noticed that there is no currency symbol in the Salon Success Standard (chapter 6) – it is just a number.

The communication we use must relate to the way the team think. Don't use percentages and definitely don't use percentages of turnover - it doesn't mean a thing.

Talk about real things – "You did 10 clients yesterday and only 2 of them will be able to do their hair this morning because the other 8 haven't got the right products. That means that 8 of the clients you did yesterday will not look as good as you want them to today – let's hope they don't tell anyone who did their hair, if it's not looking good!"

Maybe I'm wrong, but I think that is just so much more powerful than telling someone that their retail percentage is only 8%.

Remember – the archer doesn't blame the target when they miss – if your team are not motivated, if they don't get it, you must look at yourself and identify where the communication is going wrong – you can't just keep blaming them for being de-motivated.

Can you imagine how often I hear comments like this

> 66 But Alan the kids today, they are different. They don't think like we used to, they don't have the same loyalty or commitment. 99

Come on be honest, I bet some of you have said something similar yourselves.

Well, there are two choices – you could embark on a mission to turn every teenager back into how they 'used to be' or you could change the way you communicate with them!!"

Are you going to change the target or your aim?

This is happening right through the industry. Remember the fly test – we keep repeating behaviours that are getting us nowhere, particularly in the way that we are trying to motivate and communicate with our team.

Let's look at some of the things we use, to try and motivate hairdressers to be better hairdressers:

Money: Well we all like money and we would all I'm sure, like some more but that is different to being motivated by it, particularly long term. Money tends to be a good short-term motivator, particularly when you need some but it only works for the minority in something like hairdressing – a creative industry.

I can already hear some of you arguing with this, so let me put some evidence on the table for you. How do we pay people in the salon business? Mostly, it is through some sort of commission or bonus scheme. So they get more money for doing more work, selling more services or products, charging for everything and never give anything away for free, staying later, coming in earlier, working extra days, taking a client after last appointment etc!

I rest my case –

If money motivated hairdressers, we wouldn't have half of the problems that we do have.

What else do we use to try and motivate people?

Computer print-outs and percentages – I think I've made my point about these – they are just sooooo exciting to the average stylist - of course some people love them – but really, you are not going to convince me that the majority of hairdressers do!

Here's a good one – **we try to use whatever the manufacturer or distributor gives us as a free gift to excite and motivate people** and then only if we don't want the gift for ourselves! Free gifts are nice to get, but am I really going to put myself out for a dressing gown emblazoned with a manufacturers logo?!!

Finally – and I love this one – **we use whatever it is that motivates us, to try to motivate other people.** I think everybody will agree with me if I were to say that we are all different, with different personalities and attitudes – so why do we get so frustrated when other people aren't like us?

If someone doesn't like a film that you love – it is easy to respond with something like "Why not? What's the matter with you?" There is nothing the matter with them, they are just different to you.

Now ask yourself, how often do you get frustrated because your team don't share the same enthusiasm and commitment as you do.

A friend of mine who is a salon owner was very frustrated because two members of his team did not want to give up their Sunday to attend a photo shoot that he had arranged for the team. As we talked about it, he kept saying things like "I never had opportunities like this when I was their age" and "I don't understand it, it will be a brilliant day, I can't wait" and "when I arranged this I was so excited, but now I am so fed up because they don't want to do it."

Can you see what is happening here – who is this photo shoot really for? Who is the most excited person in the team and doesn't mind giving up their Sunday for it? My friend – the salon owner!

Don't just assume that whatever motivates you will automatically motivate them.

So it's the golden rule of motivation:

We are all motivated by different things and while we are at it, let me add this: Nobody's motivation is wrong, it's just who they are. If I am motivated by going home early, you can either judge me as lazy or accept that it motivates me and then use it to make me more productive. (Someone's motivation might be wrong for the job that they do however – you can't say I am wrong for wanting to go home straight after work and not be involved in training, shows and photo shoots, unless I am your art director!)

Don't blame the target if you are not getting results – change your aim

There are two other rules of motivation that are worth looking at as well:

If you accept that everybody is motivated by different things, that you have to motivate the individual – then you have to get to know your team, what turns them on, what turns them off?

Do not make the mistake though of asking what motivates them – most people don't know and they will just tell you what they think you want to hear – money, opportunities, job satisfaction etc. - Boring!

Ask them to tell you about a time recently when they felt motivated. It doesn't have to relate to work, just something that happened that made them feel good, energised and excited.

If they are struggling, get them to go back further, even as far as childhood - anything however small that gave them a kick. Once they have found something, they will find it easier. Then ask them for another one, and then one more.

They are telling you about <u>when</u> they were motivated, not what motivated them. Listen carefully and you will learn a lot about how to motivate that individual.

The final rule of motivating is the one that messes it all up! People's motivations change. Just when you thought you'd got it sussed, everything changes – of course it does – the person who never seemed to want to go home and wasn't at all bothered about what they were earning has just got married and bought a house. The target has moved and so must your aim.

If you feel that some of the stuff we have been discussing here is relevant to you, you may want to look at my second book 'the fantastic boss' .The overall focus of it is all about leadership – how to communicate with, motivate and train people to achieve fantastic results.

The Fantastic Salon's team knows why they come to work

A committed team needs to have something to commit to — you can't just expect them to be committed because you are. Create a goal with the team — it is then their goal — they start to understand why they come to work every day.

The Fantastic Salon has the right people working in it

The balance of your team is critical — you must have the right people working for you. 100% hairdressers - not 50% ones that do great hair but cause havoc everywhere else. Good recruitment and training are essential here, you can't just wish for a better team — you have to train them!

The Fantastic Salon's team are excited about what they do

Motivation is all about communication — so communicate in such a way that motivates your team to fly! Remember the 'boardroom to the changing room' — are you turning people off as fast as you are trying to turn them on?

Choose 3 goals from this chapter that you can take immediate action on:

8 DELIGHTED CLIENTS

The 'hole in the bucket'

All businesses, however good they are, will lose customers.

It's the amount of customers you lose that is the issue.

The trendy business term for this is 'churn'.

I call it the hole in the bucket!

Every salon has new clients walking through the door, some just happen to be passing, some come from your marketing and the majority through recommendation.

However they come to you, if you do not have a regular flow of new clients coming in to the salon then something is wrong, especially when you consider that most new clients are referrals.

You have all heard the old one about 'position, position, position' being the most import element of a successful service or retail business. Well of course position is important, however I know of very successful salons in dreadful positions. I travel 40 miles to my dentist – it certainly isn't a good position for me!

No, I would change it to

'referral, referral, referral'

- this being the most important element of a business like ours.

More of that later, but the point I am making is that even a half-decent salon will have new clients walking through the door every week.

Let's take a salon with 8 stylists doing just one new client per stylist every other day. That's 2.5 new clients per week, per stylist which equals 20 new clients a week – easy surely – some of you will be doing much more than this – I am purposely being conservative.

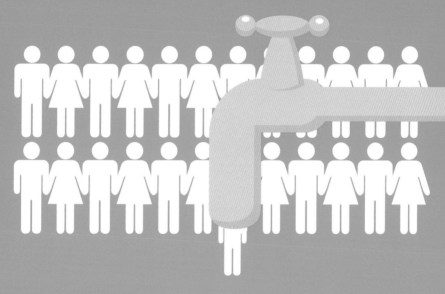

Well just 20 new clients a week is over 1,000 new clients a year!

That's a lot of people!!

Ok, let's imagine that your average client visit frequency is every 8 weeks. That means you will be getting about 6 visits a year from each client, on average.

That's an extra 6,000 visits/appointments per year!

Now, if you times that by the average client spend, let's say just 35, then that is a **potential growth of 210,000**

Which I think immediately raises the question…

Where is it?

Ok, well obviously as I have already said, you are never going to keep every client, there will always be some sort of hole in the bucket, but you really do need to find out how big yours is.

This is how you do it:

First, check out how many new clients you had over the past 12 months - your computer should be able to give you this information. If you are not yet computerised or do not collect this information manually - you must - it is critical.

Now check up what your average client visit frequency is (4,6 or 8 weeks etc.) to work out how many visits you get per client, per year on average. Divide 52 (weeks) by that figure and you will see how many visits you get per year.

Work out what your potential growth is - that is assuming you did not lose any clients at all - by multiplying your new client figure by your average visits per year by your average client spend.

Divide the answer by 52 and that is the extra sales you would be doing a week, if you had not lost any clients whatsoever - your potential growth figure.

1,000 new clients x 6 visits per year x 35 ÷ 52 = 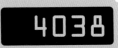 4038

Now take the sales from a 3 month period 15 months ago and compare it with your most recent three months sales - this will give your **actual** growth.

Let's say that 15 months ago you were taking 10,000 a week, and over the last three months you have been taking 11,000 a week - that is 1,000 per week actual growth.

Your hole in the bucket is the difference between those two figures – potential growth; in this case just over 4,000 and actual growth; in this case 1,000.

This salon is losing over 3,000 per week! Or just over 60 clients a month – every month!!

Once again, I strongly advise you not do this exercise near an open window in a high building!

People always ask me how big the hole should be, but it is impossible to give you a general benchmark here as there are so many variables - high passing trade, holiday spot, special occasion salon or spa, etc., all of which could mean a bigger hole in the bucket than the norm.

I prefer to look at how much I need to close the hole, in order to get the results I want. For example, to have doubled my growth over that period, I would just have close the hole in the bucket down by 20 clients - losing 40 clients a month instead of 60.

Ok, that's the hole in the bucket. If you don't monitor this, you are missing a key potential growth area.

One last thing here - can I just make the point to anybody who thinks this doesn't matter as long as you have enough new clients coming in to replace the ones you are losing – this is such a short term approach – you will run out of customers eventually.

Surely, the worst thing any service provider wants to hear is this

"I went there – ONCE!"

Be your client's 'hairdresser'

We have to create a long-term environment for our clients. We all know that the competition is so great today; you have to tie your clients into your salon – make them 'sticky' – as I say.

There is something I hear in salons all around the world that is actually sub-consciously encouraging both clients and hairdressers to think short term.

First of all though let me explain how this works:

The power of words is incredible. When we say things to people, the words that we use impact in many different ways. Firstly of course they impact at a conscious level – we all understand that – however it is the effect that they have on our sub-conscious that is perhaps most important.

For example, if I were to say,

"the window was broken"

This appears to be a simple 4 word statement which you would just acknowledge at the conscious level.

However if I was to start questioning you now, by asking whether it was a big window or a small window, is it still broken or has it been mended, what broke it etc., you could be giving me answers to those questions. So where are those answers coming from? They are coming from the 'mind movie' that you have created in your sub-conscious, without even realising it.

In order for the brain to understand words, it has to process them, which it does by creating a 'mind movie' as I call it. The most interesting thing about this is we are often completely unaware of it happening, even though it is happening all the time.

This is why words are so powerful – they impact on the subconscious and often subtly influence the way we act. The power of the influence that your sub-conscious has should never be underestimated. This is why subliminal advertising was banned – messages being included in movies and TV programmes that were flashed onto the screen so fast, our conscious mind did not register them even though our sub-conscious did.

Tests proved that when this was used in a movie theatre to sell popcorn for example, sales dramatically increased straight after it had been shown. However the audience were unaware that this was why they were buying the popcorn.

Think about hypnosis – it has nothing to with a swinging pocket watch, it is all about words - skillfully used by the hypnotist to influence our sub-conscious mind into taking action.

Interestingly, it is not just the person that you say these words to that will be affected by them – the person saying them is also getting a sub-conscious message. As we hear the words that we say to other people – those same words go into our minds as much as they go into the listener's.

Especially when you say the same thing many times a day, which in something like the service industry happens frequently - we all have our own little pet phrases that we use over and over again.

This brings me back to the point that I started all this with. What is it that I keep hearing in salons, that is creating this short-term attitude in peoples' heads?

Get rid of the word 'today'

We use this word so much. I began to notice it when I started observing 'fantastic hairdressers' at work. What were they doing differently? - Many things as you know - if you have read my first book The Fantastic Hairdresser. But I realised that they did not use the word 'today', whereas listening to other hairdressers, that word came up, over and over again.

It starts right at the beginning - with the welcome and introduction.

How often do you hear something like this in the salon:

"Hello, I'm Alan and I'm doing your hair today."

Whereas 'fantastic hairdressers' will say;

"Hello, I'm Alan and I'm your <u>hairdresser</u>."

It may seem like a small difference but it is huge. The sub-conscious message that 'today' gives is short term – 'today', whereas the message that you get from the second approach is long term.

In fact as you listen to the best performers – the people who keep their clients, they are always talking to their clients with an assumption that they will be coming back again in the future.

Here is another example;

"What are we doing with your hair today?"

Should be something like;

"How is your hair at the moment?"

Or perhaps;

"What are your long term goals for your hair?"

Get rid of the word today and replace it with questions or statements that are always assuming their relationship with you is a long term one rather than just having their hair done 'today'!

Be their hairdresser – don't just do their hair today

The best examples of this attitude that I have ever seen are from a hairdresser who many of you have heard me refer to as 'Mary'. This is not her real name, it's a pseudonym. She doesn't want me to tell people who she is, which of course I have to respect. Unfortunately, because of this I know that some people think she is a figment of my imagination. However, I assure you that this is not the case.

Mary might not be her real name, but everything else about her is very real!

I chose the name after the film 'There's something about Mary' because there is certainly 'something' about this Mary!

Everybody reading this will have different pricing structures and appointment systems, however I am sure you will all be able to appreciate how exceptional this young lady is.

She works as a stylist in a salon based in the South of England. She charges £45 for a cut and finish, working on 45 appointments, doing between 8-10 clients a day. The salon does not have a technical department as such - all stylists do their own colour work albeit with help from senior assistants.

She consistently averages £5,000 per week in takings.

She is putting £5,000 per week in the till every week!

Her average bill is £110 against a £45 hair cut!!

For every 10 of her clients that walk out of the door, 8 leave having just had colour in their hair, 9 would have at least two products in a bag and almost every client has a scalp massage and hair treatment every time they visit the salon!!!

Now that's what I call a fantastic hairdresser

How does she do it? Well obviously there are many great things she does, some of which I will discuss when we talk about 'raving clients'. However having listened to her many times, it is clear to me that it is based upon this 'long term' attitude we are talking about – I am your hairdresser, not just today, not even for just a few months – but ongoing.

Her clients are sticky, but they also trust her. She has built that trust over a period of time and now they will do almost whatever she tells them they need to do, in order to achieve what they want to achieve with their hair.

Trust is such a key thing for any service provider to be able to grow their business. You need your customers to trust you, firstly so that they will return, secondly so that they will take your advice and thirdly so that they will recommend other people to you.

It's simple –

trust is all about consistency

Think about it in other situations – we trust people who are consistent. Interestingly we might still like people who are inconsistent, but we would not entirely trust them.

I think that this is one of the reasons why a salon can maintain a relatively healthy level of business, but find it so difficult to get dramatic growth.

Clients are coming to you because they like you, because they like their hair, because you are convenient etc. But if you are not consistent, even if they choose to tolerate your in-consistencies, would they dare to recommend you?

Remember I told you earlier in the book that I say this to every one of my audiences:

"I don't question for one minute whether you are doing it right – of course you are – my only question is whether you are doing it right consistently?"

So as we have already discussed in this book, consistency is the key –

You can't just delight people on Thursdays!

It's not just consistency day to day though, you have to look at consistency throughout the team as well.

Do this little exercise for me; think of the person who lets you down the most regarding service/delight in your salon. Now understand that as you picture that person in your mind, what you are looking at is the standard of service that your salon provides!

Now you might argue with me, but it's true – if I happen to meet that person during my visit to the salon, that is what I will base my perception of the salon on. Now that's unfair of course – however we all do it.

Let's deal with consistency throughout the team first – it's simple.

Identify who these people are - they are probably a big cause of any hole in the bucket that you may have – now train them. It is no good hoping things will improve, we have to take action. That action has to start with personal development. Identify the problem, discuss it with them and then look at what needs to happen in order to change it. Again I talk about this in much more detail in The Fantastic Boss particularly when I am talking about the performance gap. However if things aren't changing, you are going to have to get tough – you can't afford to allow one or two individuals ruin the reputation of your business.

Ok, now let's go back to day-to-day consistency.

You have to be offering the same level of product, service and experience every day.

This sort of consistency can only come from your company standards. The first of these standards you need to have in place relate to your product quality – in other words – hair and/or beauty services. This is not my field anymore but it goes without saying that you need to have some sort of procedure in place to ensure that, firstly people are qualified to a certain level and then that they are constantly improving and developing those standards.
The second area relates to the service and experience your client receives. A great tool for helping you to develop service standards that have been agreed by everybody, is something I call 'walk the salon'.

Walk the salon

Get the whole team together outside your salon. Now, acting as though you are all 'one' person - a client visiting your salon, start to 'walk the salon' together as a team.

As you progress through the salon, ask them what they would expect from their experience at each stage of the journey - as if they were a client who was visiting a salon like yours, paying the same amount of money as your clients do.

There are 5 key areas in the journey through a hairdressing salon – obviously this would be slightly different in a beauty salon or spa but you will be able to work it out easily enough.

The first area is reception. Move the team from outside the salon into reception, having already noted anything that needs to change out there – messy entrance etc.

Make sure someone is making notes and then start asking the team what sort of service, what sort of experience they would want here if they were the client – waiting time, magazines, refreshments etc., how they think things should be.

Now move on to the consultation and have a similar conversation, before moving to the backwash. The final two are 'the service' in other words, whatever the client is having done and their exit.

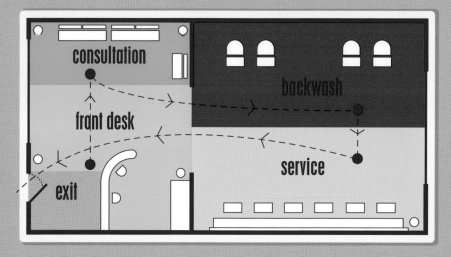

You should now have loads of things that the team have agreed need to happen. This forms the basis of your service standards which should also then form the basis of your induction training for new people.

Minimum critical standards

Finally put in place a series of standards that should enable you to aim for a level of 100% consistency in key areas.
100%?! How can you ever get 100% consistency when human beings are involved? - I hear you ask.

Well of course you're right,

if you aim for 100% you will probably fall short sometimes, however if you are not aiming for 100% then you will fall far shorter!

This will help enable you to aim for 100% consistency in key areas as well enabling you to enforce it.

Critical standards are simply the ones that you pull from all the standards that you already have and then identify as critical. For example, you might have a standard that says; any magazines in the salon should always be the current months' issue. A good standard – but not critical. What about the one that says every client should be greeted at reception as soon as they walk through the door? Now that one is critical.

Go through all of your standards and pull out between 5-7 critical standards in each key area of the salon, reception, consultation etc.

Now you have to set them at a minimum level so that you can enforce a level of consistency with each standard. For example, you may have a standard that says the phone must be answered before 4 rings – impossible to be 100% consistent and impossible to enforce as there could be a very good reason why it didn't happen.

By simply adding, 'however if for some good reason that doesn't happen, you must apologise for keeping the caller waiting' you have turned it into a minimum standard, which can now be achieved 100% of the time.

If you had a critical standard that said the client must be greeted immediately with a smile, eye contact and a verbal welcome - you once again have a standard that it is impossible to enforce 100% of the time. What if the only person who could greet a particular client is on the phone?

Leave out the verbal greeting in the minimum critical standards (that is not to say that the full standard becomes diminished – you still want a verbal greeting if at all possible) and then you'll end up with; greet the client immediately, with at least a smile and eye contact.

Once again this can be enforced as there can be no excuse for not doing it – it doesn't matter how busy everybody is, there is no reason why this can't happen.

Do this for each key area and you will end up with between 25 and 35 minimum critical standards that you can guarantee.

This will also fit onto one piece of paper - instead of the big manual folder that no-one ever looks at - and will become the core of your service standards. A level that you can achieve whatever.

Your clients should be raving – raving about you to everyone!

They are your best advert – or possibly your worst.

Everybody in this business knows that the secret to growing your client base is through recommendations and referrals. I have always said that no matter how big the marketing budget you will still always get more clients through word of mouth than by any other method.

This is where we go back to what I have just been saying about trust and also the hole in the bucket. The key for me about this whole chapter is that there is a very simple strategy that is guaranteed to give you amazing growth:

Plug the hole in the bucket and turn the tap on faster.

The consistency we have just been discussing will achieve both those things. Consistently delighting your clients, giving them a fantastic experience will certainly mean they will come back to you. But it also means they will have the confidence to recommend you - which will bring more clients in – turning the tap on faster as well as plugging the hole – which must result in dramatic growth!

The interesting thing about our business, is that it is not just what people say about us that impacts on others, (both positively or negatively remember) how they look says just as much about us.

What your client's hair looks like out there in their every day life is perhaps the biggest measurement of a fantastic hairdresser. It is not what they look like sitting in your chair in front of the mirror that makes you a fantastic hairdresser – with all our skills, professional equipment – straightening irons etc., great products at our disposal – they should look fantastic in the mirror.

No, it is what they look like in two weeks time whilst out shopping that is the key measurement of a fantastic hairdresser.

I asked 'Mary' one day, how she keeps her consistency, as it is not just the fact that she puts £5,000 a week in the till, it is that she does this consistently. The £5,000 is her average, not a figure she has hit once or twice.

I loved her answer – in fact, I think it should become a mantra for all hairdressers:

"I'm paranoid" she said "paranoid about what my clients look like – outside the salon"

Isn't that great – I think a few more hairdressers should be paranoid about what their clients look like when they are not in the salon. If they were, maybe a few more people would be walking around with professionally coloured hair as well as a great haircut and also be using the right products at home.

This is the basis of Mary's attitude; it's how she achieves such amazing results.

She is simply very clear about what her job is. She is there to make her clients look and feel fantastic, which in her mind simply means that they have to have; a great hair cut, colour in their hair, the right products in their bathroom and enjoy a relaxing scalp massage, thus benefiting from healthy hair. Finally, she makes sure they book in for their next appointment before they leave.

Here is something interesting that I learnt from her regarding this:

Always suggest re-booking whilst the client is in the chair rather than waiting until they get to the desk.

Think about the psychology behind this – at the desk they are handing over money, sometimes a lot of money and you are effectively saying "do you want to do that again in six weeks?"

It's not surprising that a lot of people say that they will 'leave it for now'. Suggesting re-booking whilst they are in the chair though is different – they are enjoying themselves – or should be – so therefore feel that they would like to repeat this experience again in six weeks time.

The perfect client

All of this culminates in something that I call the 'perfect client'. It is simply focusing on what we want walking out of the salon door every day – perfect clients.

Ask your team; what is the perfect advert for us – what sort of client is going to get us new business by how they look as well as what they say?

They know – they will tell you. You may have to prompt them a bit but I guarantee that they will not disagree – they can't.

There are 6 elements to a perfect client – it is someone who has:

A great hair cut, beautiful colour, regularly treated healthy hair, great products in their bathroom, re-booked their next appointment

and finally…

Is raving about you to everyone!

Start measuring perfect clients – you may be surprised how few you are doing but you will also be amazed how many more you start to get over a period of time when you and the team start focusing on them.

The more perfect clients you send out the door, the more people who are walking around out there looking and feeling fantastic – that must mean you are doing a great job! Oh, and by the way your sales will go through the roof!

The second consultation

After Mary told me about her paranoia – I asked her another obvious question that just had to be asked.

"How do you do it?" I asked "How do you turn a £45 haircut into a £110 average bill?"

She laughed and with a cheeky glint in her eye, thinking she was being funny, she pinpointed the absolute key to it all.

"Well it's not quite a simple as that Alan" she said, " it's not as if they come in expecting to spend £45 and go out spending £110 – it takes me a good six to nine months to train my clients up to standard!"

It takes 6 to 9 months to train up her clients!

That's it I thought – back to this long term approach again – she is not trying to get her clients to have everything 'today' but she is determined that they will all be perfect clients eventually.

When I listen to her and other fantastic hairdressers it is immediately clear how they do what they do – they give a second consultation.

The first consultation is the same for everybody – it lasts about 5 minutes (if they are lucky) and is focused on what is going to happen today.

The second consultation can be anything up to 30 minutes as it takes place whilst you are doing their hair. It deals with the future – long term planning. It gives the stylist the opportunity to advise and suggest whatever they feel is needed, to help the client achieve their 'hair goals'. It also allays any fears that the client might have had from the stylist rushing to discuss this on their first consultation. It is a no risk situation for them, so they are much more open to new ideas and suggestions.

To explain how this works, let me point out how your salon is already doing this.

If a client came into the salon tomorrow and told you that she was getting married in nine months time – what would happen?

You would firstly find out what her 'hair goals' were – how does she want her hair for the wedding?

Then you would start planning long term with her.

Let me ask you some questions:

Will that bride walk down the aisle with colour in her hair? YES!

Will she have the right products in her suitcase as she sets off on honeymoon? YES!

Will she have had some treatments leading up to the big day? YES!

You see, we are doing it already - it is just that Mary does it with every client, not just the brides.

The more people you send out the door looking and feeling fantastic, the more business they will generate for you – it's simple!

The Fantastic Salon's clients are sticky

Measure your hole in the bucket – are you losing too many clients? Make your clients sticky, plug the hole with consistency and delight and not only will you plug the hole, you will also turn the tap on faster.

The Fantastic Salon's clients trust their salon

Trust comes from consistency – consistency comes from standards – review your standards – do a 'walk the salon' and then enforce them. Remember, a standard not being enforced is not a standard and even more importantly, one standard not being enforced means you lose all of them!

The Fantastic Salon's clients are raving

Turning the tap on faster means more new clients through word of mouth – or as I call it – raving clients – raving about you and your salon to everybody they meet. Improve consistency, increase delight and your clients will be raving – about you!

Choose 3 goals from this chapter that you can take immediate action on:

UN IQU

MAR K

JE 9

T ING

The 30 second marketing course

Ready for the 30 second marketing course?

Ok then, here we go…..

Tell your clients and your prospective clients about all the things that you do!

That didn't even take 30 seconds – I will have to re-name it the 10 second marketing course.

The point I am trying to make here, is that before you get involved with expensive and sophisticated marketing techniques, start by simply making sure people know about all the services that you offer, products that you sell, training that you do etc.

A good salon does so much good stuff that in many cases not even their regular clients are aware of it, let alone prospective new clients.

I've heard so many stories about this over the years;

Long term clients who are surprised to discover that you offer beauty services

Clients who think semi-permanent/direct colour is only available as a home application product, unaware that they can have this done in the salon

Clients who are surprised to find out that they don't have to have a full head of lights – that they could even just have 5 or so packets in their fringe

The fantastic salon doesn't keep secrets

Salons that offer free parking but don't tell anyone

Salons that invest heavily in training their team in customer service – but don't tell anyone

I couldn't even begin to count how many salons have closed for the day to send their entire team on one of my seminars, or even pay for me to come to them.

However, I could count on just two hands the amount who made a PR story out of it for their local press. It is a huge commitment that you very rarely see any other business make. Close down for a whole day to train the team - when was the last time you saw a notice on the door of a bank, retail outlet, gym, florist etc., saying they were 'closed today for team training'?

We do some pretty special stuff as an industry sometimes, but we don't tell enough people about it.

If you don't already, think about entering local business competitions – I guarantee you will do well, if only because of the pre-conceptions of the judges – they will be amazed that a 'hairdressing salon' is so switched on and professional.

A customer of mine ran an incredibly successful marketing campaign a few years back. It had a big impact on his new client numbers and even today he is still getting new clients from it. People who didn't take up the service he was offering at that time had still remembered it and come back at a later date.

It was a multi-media campaign. He used local press advertising and PR, radio, posters etc. His message was everywhere and the response was amazing. The phone didn't stop ringing. People were coming into the salon asking "Is this the place where…"

Not only that though, it became a very 'sticky' campaign - a very high percentage of the new clients who tried this service turned into long term regular customers.

Sounds amazing doesn't it – what on earth was it that he was telling everybody about?

Free Consultations!!
Free Consultations!!!
Free Consultations!!

FREE CONSULTATIONS!

That's it – something that any salon offers. In fact, he even had friends who ran salons locally say to him, "What are you doing? We all do that."

"I know" he answered. "I'm just letting everybody know we do it."

When I use that story to teach marketing outside of our business sector, so many people say to me that they didn't know they could just walk into a salon and get a free consultation. Even the ones that do know say that they would still be more likely to go into a salon if they were 'invited' in for it.

Have a team meeting and do a brain storming session on all the great things that you offer as a salon that if you are honest a high percentage of your clients and thus a much higher percentage of your prospective clients don't know about. Now base a marketing campaign around telling people about all you offer.

Marketing does not have to be tacky and all the best and most exclusive brands market themselves.

Don't keep secrets – tell the world how fantastic you are!

What is it you want people to know about you? With marketing, what you are really doing is creating a reputation, a perception of your business as well as telling people what's going on.

This is where we get strategic again – marketing shouldn't be random – it must have a purpose and the results must be measured.

Remember strategy; where are you now, where are you going and how are you going to get there?

Here is another way of looking at it. I use this whenever I am creating a marketing strategy, planning a training session/meeting or writing a book.

WHY?   WHO?   WHAT?

The order of these three questions is critical. In fact, I find that most of the time, if things don't work it's either because these questions haven't all been answered, or the order in that they were asked, was wrong.

Why? – has to be the first question. Why are you doing what you are doing – what are you trying to accomplish, what are the goals and objectives?

You are doing a community hair and fashion show – why? Because it's fun, to motivate the team, get new clients, introduce existing clients to new services? Why are you doing this show?

This is a great example of when the questions are being asked in the wrong order, or not asked at all.

Too many times people go straight to question 3 – What? – what are we going to do? All the focus and attention is spent on what you are going to do for the show, being creative etc., without having first identified why you are doing it!

You are having an open evening – why? – What are the objectives?

The fantastic salon has a message

You are placing an advert in the local press – why? – What do you want to achieve with it?

You are changing your opening hours – why?

I think that sometimes in such a creative business – we can be so un-creative. I don't mean with hair of course – I am talking about the other stuff - remember – the 50% rule. Particularly with marketing. I sometimes look at the way many salons advertise for new team members – where is the creativity? I find that a lot of the time, people are picking up on ideas from other salons or seminars and implementing them without questioning - why?

I used to be a partner in a salon that took the first appointment at 7.30am. I will always remember a guy who proudly told me he was now doing this as well.

"Why?" I asked him.

He look panicked for a moment and said "Because you are - doesn't it work?"

"Yes" I replied " It works for us, but why are you doing it?"

Our salon was in a business district where you couldn't get a parking space if you arrived after 8.00 am. We were next to a gym that ran an aerobic class at 6.30am!! We knew why we took a 7.30 appointment. However this guys' salon was in a nice market town in the Midlands where possibly the only people around at that time in the morning were commuters or street cleaners.

I wasn't saying that he shouldn't open at 7.30, it was just that I wanted him to tell me he had carried out some research first - spoken to other local businesses, commuters, clients etc. And that the results of his research had told him it might be a good idea - rather than just doing it because we did!

The first question is: Why? – Stick to this discipline and the results you get from your marketing strategies, team meetings, training sessions etc., will improve dramatically.

I think it is worth noting here that marketing is not just about the usual stuff. It is everything and anything that sends a message out there, about how you operate. The way you lead your team becomes marketing, as people will notice and comment on good leadership (or bad)!! Your opening hours, customer delight policies, refreshment menu, prices, reception area etc., are all saying things about your business and therefore need to be recognised as marketing.

Why did you choose that reception desk – because you liked it or because it was welcoming?

The first question is always – WHY? You have to know your business - it's weaknesses and strengths. Use a swot analysis, do your research, use your computer - then you can ensure that any marketing you are doing is for the right reasons.

Having identified why you are doing something, the next question is – who?

Who is going to get this message – who is it aimed at, or who is listening?

You must know your market before you decide what marketing you are going to do. You know what you are trying to achieve, now ask yourself - with who? Existing clients, new clients, do you want to extend your catchment area, change your current client profile, are you recruiting, who is in the audience for your show – hairdressers or members of the public, etc?

Now finally you can ask the last question – if you know why you are doing something, if you know who your audience is, then now and only now, can you start to think about what you are going to do.

What is your message and what is the best way to get that message across?

A message, any message is only effective if it gets to its intended recipient.

You are in the battle for business, but who are your competitors and where is the battlefield?

Your competitors are not just other salons, your competition is anyone who is after your client's disposable income.

Clothes shops, shoe shops, restaurants, bars, travel agents etc.

We all have an amount of money left over that is for us and we have to apportion it between all those things and more. This means that we are sometimes making a decision about what would be the best way to spend that money. Perhaps I can't afford to have colour in my hair and buy those new shoes this month – so which will it be?

That's why we have to be good at what we do. We have to be so good that someone chooses their hair colour rather than shoes!

If you understand that this is the competition, then it easier to understand where the battlefield is – where will the battle between colour and shoes take place?

It's in the clients' head – the battlefield is in peoples' minds. Therefore, if you want to get on to the battlefield, (let's face it you don't stand much chance of winning if you are not even 'out there'!) then you have to get into their heads.

The 'so what' rule

I love this little rule – I use it all the time and I would suggest that you do as well. Look at any marketing, PR, press releases etc., that you do and ask yourself, "can I say 'so what' to this?"

The best way to get into this is to start using it with the marketing that is all around us. In fact just look at the average salon's advertising – what is the message? Is it marching powerfully onto the battlefield or limping in at the edge?

Does it get you thinking? As a client, would it have a powerful enough message for you to make a decision or is it just telling you that there is a salon on the high street called 'x' and this is their phone number?

Is the message unique – is it different, are they telling you what you know already or just what you would expect anyway?

In other words, 'so what?!'

The fantastic salon has a message - a message that is focused, being delivered to the right people and finally a message that makes people take some action.

Now all we have to do is get the message delivered!

Your marketing strategy should be based around 5 key areas.

Advertising
PR
The internet
Internal marketing
Active marketing

Advertising

This is all about budget. If you have a big marketing budget, then a strong, unique message delivered via an advertising medium can be effective. However, this is only if you have money to spend, as the only way advertising works is with a drip, drip campaign – consistently reminding people of your message over a period of time. Of course this can be very expensive. Occasional random adverts, just appearing once or twice are a complete waste of money.

You have to understand how advertising works. Imagine you are at home watching a movie and an advert for a new chocolate bar comes on the screen. You don't just jump out of your chair and rush down the road to buy it. It registers with you, you think to yourself "that looks nice" then the movie starts again and you forget about it.

A couple of days later, you see an advert for the bar in a magazine. "Must try one of those" you say to yourself, and then turn the page.

It might be weeks later that you see the bar in a shop and say: "Oh there's that chocolate. Think I'll get some." - That's how advertising works.

Turn it around and look at it from another point of view. Would you expect your clients to stop coming to you and start visiting another salon just because they saw one advert from that other salon? Of course not. So why would other salon's clients come to you?

What happens is this: One day a client is fed up with their salon or can't get an appointment. Then they will think, "Now where is that salon I keep seeing advertised? Maybe I'll give them a try." Again, that's how advertising works.

So my advice to you is that unless you have a big enough budget to be consistent, don't advertise unless you either have something specific to say or you are using an advertorial. (This is is when you are paying for the space but are also able to write an editorial for people to read) - If you do this well and are creative with it, then it can be worthwhile.

The same is true of direct mail. A successful direct mail campaign is one that will give you a 1-2% response rate. If you can't afford to do a big one – leave it alone.

PR

This used to be the golden egg of local marketing until the local press started to get wise to it. It is increasingly difficult to get free publicity therefore I strongly suggest that you use a professional PR to help you.

However, let's go back to the 'who' question. Is it industry PR you need, or consumer? I find many salons using industry PR's to get their pictures in industry magazines but are not investing in getting their message to their clients. What are the objectives? Who are you trying to get to? Then decide on the best way to get there!

Be creative

The best way to communicate effectively is to put yourself in the other parties' shoes. With PR, you have to sell your message to the publication before you can get it to your market. What is going to make your story stand out from all the others they see? Providing a press release as a ready-made story for example will have a much better chance of getting in. Use headlines - it's how the media sells to us.

For example, sending a few pictures to a local paper and telling them this is your summer collection will not have as much impact as:

…followed by a ready-made article including your pictures.

The Internet

What is your online personality like? Like it or not, you have to accept that the consumer of today makes a lot of their decisions on how you look on line. I certainly do when I am booking hotels, restaurants, spa's etc.

First of all, if you do not have a website you are losing lots of potential business. Secondly, if your web site is not consistent with your message, people won't get the message.

The biggest mistake I see with websites is that they are put together between yourself and a web designer, without any input from an online marketing expert. Much as I suggest you use professional PR, I also suggest that you use an on-line marketing expert. This whole area is a minefield if you don't know what you are doing and you can waste a lot of money creating a lovely website that nobody goes to.

Internal marketing

Internal marketing is when the delivery of your message is focused on your existing clients.

Any marketing strategy must include internal marketing to develop your client count and value. Client education evenings, offering complimentary services to fill appointment gaps, client information sheets, newsletters etc., staff incentives, fun ideas to focus peoples' minds - "ask me about..." etc.

Use your database for newsletters, birthday cards, special promotions etc. You should also be focusing on lapsed clients – a simple letter to those clients who have not visited you in the last few months, including a gift voucher for use in the salon on their next visit (personally I much prefer gift vouchers to discount vouchers – same thing, just sounds much more appealing). What do you have to lose? – They are not visiting you at the moment so anything you get from it, is a bonus.

A successful way of introducing new clients to the salon and particularly to new stylists is a hair advice day/ afternoon /evening, where you book people in for free consultations.

Bring a friend promotions; capitalising on the strength of recommendation, working out a promotional deal (gift voucher preferably) for both the new client recommended and the existing client who recommended them. Make sure that you get the client to identify who they are going to give it to.

Active Marketing

Active marketing is simply actively getting out into your community and delivering the message first hand. It is cost effective and so ideal if you do not have much budget. However you will have to invest a lot of time – nobody said it would be easy!

Prepare a one hour talk aimed at increasing awareness to the importance of image in business today - obviously featuring on hair. Then contact local businesses, hotels, schools, hospitals etc., with a view to giving the presentation to them. Don't just write to them though – these guys have loads of stuff landing on their desks every day. Find out who you need to speak to and make an appointment. In most cases one of the key strengths in your business is you – your passion and energy – so let people see it.

Prepare a corporate package including discount, grooming talks, newsletter etc., for local companies in conjunction with this. Once again - make appointments.

Satellites

This is a great way of increasing your catchment area. Look through your client records and see which areas you are getting a few clients from that are currently outside of your direct catchment area. Now target those areas - maybe do a hair show for a local charity, support local schools etc. If you then add some strong internal marketing by targeting those few clients that are travelling and offer them an incentive for getting new clients in from that area, you will start to grow your catchment area.

If you have clients coming from specific areas you are interested in targeting, speak to them - they could prove good contacts. Do the same with clients from local businesses that you want to hit.

Hair Parties

Look at the success of party plan marketing – it works.

Party plan marketing works because it's not the company organising it, it's someone's friend. I am sure you have all been to something like this, however just in case, it works like this: The party organiser (a client of yours) arranges for say - 10 people to come to a hair party they have arranged at your salon on a given evening. The organiser will have some incentive such as 'x' amount of free hairdressing services.

All you do is provide some wine and nibbles and prepare an evening that will give them some general advice on their hair. It works well if you split them into groups of 3 or 4 and then do individual consultations within the group. Remember they are friends and will often help you to do your job by egging their friend on, to try something new. It is very open and relaxed - no fear for the client, as you are not doing their hair, you're just chatting about it. They love it -

How many times have you been caught at a party, by someone who finds out what you do and then spends all night talking about their hair?

Finally, finish the evening by offering them a gift voucher if they book their appointment tonight. You will book lots of appointments I guarantee, as well selling a lot of product - as you will obviously be recommending loads!

This obviously works well for new clients but a similar type of thing can be used to educate existing clients as to different services, colour etc.

All of these will give you the opportunity to introduce the other members of the team to new clients. This will also increase the client's awareness as to what your salon offers and in turn, help to build the team's clientele.

Co-operative marketing

Set up promotions with other like-minded companies, such as gift vouchers in with the card that the florist attaches to their flowers. Add hair care advice and information on sun protection products in with travel tickets from the travel agents.

Restaurants, clothes shops etc., - there are many opportunities.

Marketing strategy

Much of what we have discussed here is not costly but it will need spending some time on, to do it right.

Create a marketing strategy for the year - having identified your objectives, market and relevant messages. Now build into that strategy the best ways to deliver those messages using some or all of the 5 mediums I have suggested here – advertising, PR, the internet, internal marketing and finally active marketing.

The Fantastic Salon doesn't keep secrets

The 30 second marketing course – tell everybody what you do! It is sometimes as simple as that – brainstorm with your team a list of all the things that you offer in your salon, all the things that you do, that a high percentage of your clients probably don't know about – and then tell them all about it!

The Fantastic Salon has a message

Marketing is about creating a reputation for your business – what reputation do you want to create – how do you want people to perceive you? Are you getting that message across with your marketing – are you getting into peoples' heads or is the response to your marketing simply "so what?!"

The Fantastic Salon makes sure everyone gets the message

Now all you have to do is get the message out there. Create a marketing strategy based around these 5 media – Advertising, PR, The Internet, Internal Marketing and Active Marketing. You don't have to spend fortunes – be creative and get out there – make it happen rather than just sitting there waiting for people to walk through the door.

Choose 3 goals from this chapter that you can take immediate action on:

The fantastic revolution

I believe there is a revolution occurring in the salon industry and I think that we are right smack bang in the middle of it now.

I think we are going through possibly the biggest changes we have encountered since Vidal Sassoon introduced cutting hair differently. I am sure you all know your industry history and appreciate the awesome impact that Vidal had on this business.

I can't think of many people who have single-handedly changed an entire industry

Bill Gates would be one, but there aren't many.

So why am I comparing what is happening currently to what happened in the 60's and had such a big impact across the world?

It's to do with the way the changes that Vidal started, travelled through the industry.

It started with a small band of salons and hairdressers that were so far ahead of everyone else in what they were doing. The rest of the world looked on and said one of three things;

It was either:

"I've got to be part of this"

or

"I should be part of this, but...."

or

"I'm not changing – why should I?!"

Well I think we all know what happened to anyone who said the latter - either their business died or their clients did!

Of course, anyone who said the first one enjoyed being part of the revolution that occurred.

It is the second one that interests me the most:

"I should be part of this, but...."

There would have been many things said that followed the word 'but' – time issues, fear of change, lack of knowledge, ego etc. However eventually they must have all come on board, otherwise the changes that were happening would not have been sustained.

In fact, although (quite rightly) the credit goes to the people who started it all - from Vidal, through to all the people who were committed to educating people around the world -

the real impact came when the second group put their fears etc., behind them and realised that they had to take action, they had to change.

That is exactly where we are now in the journey we are on, from hairdressing salon to hairdressing business.

For the last 15 - 20 years, the 'pathfinders' have been learning new skills and techniques whilst thinking differently about their business. The results have been incredible – there are salons out there that are making sales and profit that would have been perceived as impossible, only a few years ago.

But the revolution is gaining pace and what I am noticing currently is that the second group – the "I should but…" group - are now joining in. New salons that open understand it's a new world, existing salons are rapidly learning great new stuff and putting it into action – large, medium, small – it doesn't make any difference. - One of our customers who has just 3 stylists in her salon including herself, has committed to over £10,000 worth of training and consultancy this year!

"Just because my business is small, that doesn't mean it can't be fantastic" she tells me – and she's right!

All this means two things:

Firstly, if you are not changing, if you are not moving, if you are standing there on the beach with your feet stuck in the sand, your arms folded resolutely, refusing to move whilst watching the waves crash in – then you have to realise that the waves aren't going to stop. Like it or not the world is changing and you have a simple choice. Get on the surfboard and start riding those waves of change or stay there on the beach and drown – because that is what will happen – as it did to those salons that did not change the way they did hair.

Secondly, what if you are one of the first group - the businesses that realised this change many years ago? Well this is a critical time for you. You have had it your own way for quite a while now but watch out, people are catching you up. As we have already discussed in the book, a lot of the creative and innovative stuff you were doing before anyone else, is now the norm. Start thinking about what you have to do, to keep your advantage as all around you race to catch up.

Remember if you want change – change something

Think about the key points that have impacted on you in this book and ask yourself; what are you going to do about it - what do you have to change?

- Has your business become 'systems without passion?'
- Do you need to get the balance back?
- Are you doing it right - consistently?
- Do you need to take the fly test?
- Are you in the boardroom or the changing room?
- Are you communicating in a way that is motivating your team?
- Do you have a revolutionary strategy or are you just driving around?
- Are you focused on profit or just on sales?
- Are your team committed or just nodding wisely?
- Are you delighting your clients or just serving them?
- Is your marketing unique or 'so what'?

And finally,

- Are you a good salon or a fantastic salon?

➡ Basically it all boils down to one thing, being good is no longer enough — it's time to step up to FANTASTIC!

Be part of the 'fantastic' revolution!!

The fantastic revolution

Ask yourself now – do you want a fantastic salon or just a good one?

Well if the answer is a 'fantastic' one then what are you going to do about it?

Remember – even if you currently do have a fantastic salon, the world is littered with companies who were 'once' fantastic – remember the 'Total Life Concept' – it's easy to slip into the centre if you are not out there on the edge - growing, changing, learning, moving, innovating, creating etc., all of the time.

I finish every seminar I do with these three questions so let me finish this book the same way:

Have you enjoyed it? I hope so.

Has it been worthwhile? Have you learnt something? Great!

Then finally – What are you going to do about it?

It's up to you -

it always has been

and

it always will be

It's not learning that changes things it's the action you take with what you learn that makes the difference

If you want change – change something!

Write down three things that have had the most impact on you from reading this book and then make a commitment to yourself to do something about it. If you get the chance — please log on to our website at www.fantastichairdresser.com and send us a mail with these three things — it's great for us to know we have helped in some small way — have fun,

Alan

Want to know more about what else we can do for you and your business?

Please visit our web site at

www.fantastichairdresser.com

- for more information on Alan's other books,

The Fantastic Hairdresser and The Fantastic Boss

You can also find out how to book Alan for 'in house' consultancy/training and conference speaking or how to use our on-line learning Academy as well as learn more about the unique, industry acclaimed Fantastic Hairdresser Ambassadors' System

Alternatively, please feel free to contact us at:

The Fantastic Hairdresser Company

Barley Mow Centre
10 Barley Mow Passage
Chiswick
W4 4PH
+ 44 (0) 20 8996 1644
info@fantastic-hairdresser.co.uk

For all press enquiries:

Shirley Dunmall
Shirley Dunmall Public Relations

Email: shirley@sdpr.co.uk

Other contact information:

Book design by: bluw creative

Garden Studios
11-15 Betterton Street
Covent Garden
London
WC2H 9BP
+44 (0) 20 7470 8701
www.bluw.co.uk

Also in the 'Fantastic' series...

£9.99

£12.99

Please turn the page for a taster from these...

Assuming you have decided to be a fantastic hairdresser, it's time to move on from the foundations which we have dealt with in the first part of the book. Start to look at the characteristics of a Fantastic Hairdresser, and the action you can take to achieve that goal.

I have worked in this industry for 25 years now, and have been privileged to meet and work with some really fantastic hairdressers. All of whom I have been able to learn from.

It was really difficult to pick the characteristics that I felt were the keys. I have narrowed it down to seven, but feel free to add your own if you think I have missed any.

THE FANTASTIC HAIRDRESSER HAS PASSION

It has to start here, because if you don't have a passion for what you do, you can never be fantastic at it. You will learn later that passion for what you do all boils down to how you perceive your job.

THE FANTASTIC HAIRDRESSER GIVES DELIGHT

A fantastic hairdresser will be judged on many things, but surely the most important measurement is if your clients are delighted with you, and what you do for them. That's why I call it customer delight, not customer service.

THE FANTASTIC HAIRDRESSER INSPIRES PEOPLE

If you have passion, knowledge and confidence, then now it is time to look at the most important skill of all - communication. This is not just as a hairdresser, but in life. This skill is so critical to us as human beings, yet I still find it amazing how few people take the time to consciously develop this.

Characteristics of a fantastic hairdresser

THE FANTASTIC HAIRDRESSER IS AN AMBASSADOR

The fantastic hairdresser is an ambassador for themselves, their salon and the industry. Acting in a professional manner in terms of appearance and behaviour will truly set you apart. You must also recognise that even as a fantastic hairdresser, you need other people. You can't do it on your own, and it's so much more fun as part of a successful team.

THE FANTASTIC HAIRDRESSER IS A PERFORMER

I put this next as I often feel that there are people out there with a passion for their job as well as having the right skills and knowledge, but who are not achieving what they should be because of a lack of confidence in themselves. This is one of the biggest barriers we face in taking the action we need to.

THE FANTASTIC HAIRDRESSER IS ALIVE INSIDE

We all need motivation, and there is nothing better than a pat on the back or a 'thank you' when it is needed.

However you cannot pass over the responsibility for motivation completely, to other people. We have to learn to motivate ourselves if we really want to succeed. Every fantastic hairdresser I have ever met is a positive person.

They have their up's and down's like everybody does, but they understand that they have to move past the bad moments and look forward to the future positively, rather than get caught up in all the staffroom moaning.

THE FANTASTIC HAIRDRESSER IS STILL LEARNING

Obviously passion isn't enough on its own, and has to be backed up by the skills and knowledge to do the job. Clearly these have to be at a high standard, but most importantly as we have already discussed, it is an ongoing commitment to developing that knowledge and those skills.

To do this we have to be creative. Not only is creativity a pre-requisite for this job, but as we have already discussed in the Total Life Concept, it is essential for surviving life today let alone achieving high levels of success. Creativity is simply about having the courage to be wrong, to give your ideas oxygen, let them breathe. Get that idea out of your head and give it a go.

the
fantastic
hairdresser

Austin-Smith

Assuming you have decided to be fantastic at what you do, then it's time to move on from the foundations which we dealt with in the first part of the book. Start to look at the characteristics of a Fantastic 'Boss' and the action you can take to achieve that goal.

I have been working with and learning from fantastic bosses for 25 years now. The interesting thing is, what really makes the difference, are the things that are so often overlooked. In researching this book, I spoke at length with many fantastic managers, and perhaps more importantly, to a large cross section of team members in different types of jobs and industries.

When I added their views to my own, it started to become obvious which characteristics were the keys. I have narrowed it down to the eight that we mostly agreed upon, but feel free to add your own if you think I have missed any.

THE FANTASTIC 'BOSS' KNOWS WHAT THEY ARE DOING

Every great manager I have ever worked with has the same understanding. They are clear about what their job is – why they are really doing what they do every day. Quite simply it's about getting results out of people. When you understand that, your priorities start to change.

THE FANTASTIC 'BOSS' IS A LEADER

Leadership is all about attitude – the leaders' attitude towards their team. If you believe your people are great, then you get great people. The fantastic 'boss' knows that this isn't enough though. People need direction, inspiration and motivation as well as consistent standards to work towards.

THE FANTASTIC 'BOSS' TRAINS PEOPLE

Delegation doesn't save time; it takes time to delegate properly. Building a team of people who are motivated, skilled and committed to what they are doing, will mean a lot of time spent on development. The fantastic 'boss' understands that success will come from coaching people - developing people's strengths to help them fly.

THE FANTASTIC 'BOSS' COMMUNICATES TO MOTIVATE

Communication is one of the most important skills in life. It is certainly one of the most important, if not the most important skill a manager ever has. Motivation is all about communication and great communication is all about understanding:- Understanding other people, their point of view, the position they've taken; in order for you to communicate effectively with them.

THE FANTASTIC 'BOSS' MANAGES THEMSELVES

How can we expect to manage other people, if we are not in control of ourselves? The fantastic 'boss' knows that to do the important stuff – communication, motivation etc., they have to have time. The only way to get more time, is to take control of the 24 hours a day we all have available to us.

THE FANTASTIC 'BOSS' LOVES CHANGE

We live in a fast changing world, whether you like it or not. The fantastic 'boss' today is one who is not afraid of change, who is creative, innovative, always learning, and most of all prepared to fail! If you are not failing – you are not doing anything!

THE FANTASTIC 'BOSS' IS TRUSTED

Of all the different characteristics that people mentioned when I was researching this book, trust came out highest, being listed as critically important by 95% of the people I spoke to. So what is it that makes someone trustworthy? Consistency. It is not enough to be a fantastic 'boss' some of the time, you have to do it consistently.

THE FANTASTIC 'BOSS' LOVES SUCCESS

The fantastic 'boss' wants to be successful of course, but they understand that their success comes from the team. The higher your team fly, the higher you will. Use 'The Formula' to pull it all together and achieve the success that you all want. However, remember you can't do it on your own, you need your team and you must reward them – give credit – don't take it!

The rest of this book has a chapter devoted to each of these characteristics, with useable tools and understandings that will help you on your journey towards being a fantastic 'boss'.

the
fantastic
'boss'

Austin-Smith

About the author...

Alan Austin-Smith started his hairdressing career with Vidal Sassoon in New Bond St, London, at the age of 16. Later he left Sassoon's to join Glemby International as Creative Director, based in Fenwick's, New Bond St. The next stage of his career started when he joined L'Oreal as a Technical Consultant before becoming Technical Manager.

After 7 years with L'Oreal, Alan decided to start up a company providing business training and support for salons, with his current business partner Carolyn Field (also a hairdresser – they met whilst working for Sassoon's) to whom he was married at the time. Since divorced, they have proved the value of great communication and personal life skills, as not only have they remained great friends and committed parents to their two children Craig and Samantha, their continued business partnership is the foundation of the success that they now enjoy.

Having also run their own salon whilst Alan was at L'Oreal, their enormous experience and passion for the salon business runs throughout everything the Fantastic Hairdresser Company does.

Providing the very best, business and team development support for forward thinking salons is what they are all about and they pride themselves on their amazing client base which includes almost anybody who is anybody in the UK and Irish hairdressing industry as well as many top international clients.

The Fantastic Hairdresser book was published to great industry acclaim in 2003 and has gone on to be one of the best selling books in our industry. This was followed by the Fantastic Boss in 2005, before the Fantastic Salon - published in 2007.

With an on-line learning website – the Fantastic Hairdresser Academy and the ground breaking Ambassador Programme, (an in-salon training system designed to ensure that all team members are systematically taught the 'other 50%' of being a fantastic hairdresser) Alan and Carolyn really do practice what they preach.

"No matter how good you are, no matter what success you have achieved, you must always be creating new ideas, learning new things and achieving dynamic growth - moving forward all of the time."

With a new on-line service coming soon plus an intensive live training version of the Fantastic Salon, this exciting approach continues – watch this space!

"The Ambassador Programme is like the 'Mr Muscle' of the hairdressing industry – it just unblocks everything. Suddenly our teams have come alive, a switch has gone on, they really get it!"
Gaynor Hodge
National Franchise Director, Toni & Guy

"We have seen progressive changes ever since Alan first came to the salon a few years ago. Our pre-bookings this year for October are up 50% but there is also the effect it's had on the team - they are all so keen!"
Barbara McNaughton-Khattri
Salon Owner – Elements

"Alan's training brings a fresh approach to personal development, specifically addressing common challenges within our industry"
Charles Worthington